C000240630

Underdogs

the fight to save South Africa's wild dogs

underdogs

the fight to save South Africa's wild dogs

For Hayley,

Best Wishes

Neil Aldridge

Written and photographed by Neil Aldridge

Photographs & text © Neil Aldridge (2011)
Cartography © NatureBureau
Published edition © NatureBureau

All rights reserved. No part of this publication may be reproduced, stored in a retrieval system or transmitted, in any form or by any means, electronic, mechanical, photocopying, recording or otherwise, without the prior written permission of the copyright owners.

British-Library-in-Publication Data
A catalogue record for this book is available from the British Library

ISBN 978-1-874357-49-0

First published in 2011

Publisher Pisces Publications
Pisces Publications is the imprint of NatureBureau, 36 Kingfisher Court, Hambridge Road, Newbury, Berkshire RG14 5SJ
www.naturebureau.co.uk

Design Neil Aldridge
Proofreading Wendy Collinson & John Power
Printing & Binding Information Press, Oxford

All photographs property of the author with the exception of African Wild Dog, page 16, courtesy of Peter Neville.

www.conservationphotojournalism.com

Contents

***Ever alert** (left): Stellar, the charismatic alpha female of the Venetia Limpopo pack, learnt from painful past experience to remain alert for mortal enemies even when sleeping through the heat of the day in thick mopane bush.*

Foreword

By Professor Peter Neville

Animal Behaviourist,

University of Miyazaki, Japan

and The Ohio State University, USA

One of the best photos I ever took was a blur, something most photographers would have trashed at first sight. It encapsulated everything I had learned and come to admire about African wild dogs since my first encounter with this astonishing predator. The dog was hunting at a fast trot and merging superbly with the autumnal mopane bush, the white flashes of his tail standing out in the morning light. A painted dog in appearance but a hunting dog on a mission, with friends nearby fanning out through the bush to startle some inattentive impala – a quarry that would be killed and consumed in an instant and carried back to the den to feed the alpha female and her pups.

For a biologist, this was heaven. The circle of life was going on before my very eyes. It was a life-altering chance to watch those pups grow and learn how to survive under the watchful eyes of their family. The pups were where all the energy of the hunt ended up. Some of the adults even worked so hard to feed the pups that they themselves became thin. The experience taught me that the most important members of the group are the young and it is the pups that define what it means to apply Darwin's great theory of the passing of genes through time and space.

I work with domestic dogs for the most part, treating behaviour problems between them and their owners. I have a million tales to tell of labradors and Jack Russells but I have learned more about canine behaviour from watching African wild dogs than from all of them. Everyone knows that pet dogs can be fun, that's why we keep them as pets. Biologists tell us that all behaviour has a purpose, that animals like wild dogs have evolved to ensure successful hunting and reproduction, that animals in the wild should not waste time or energy on frivolous activity because they cannot afford the risk when they have no owners to ensure their welfare. Yet, I am one of the lucky few to have seen the

humour that pervades wild dog family interactions – the playful wrestling of the pups and one adult dog's spontaneous goading of another, just like my kids do and like I did with my parents.

Such humour has a purpose. It keeps morale high and develops kinship. This chance to have fun for its own sake is one of the benefits of being a social predator. Eating food that is rich in energy means that they have the time to amuse themselves. For me, wild dogs are at their wonderful best when they are being just that – efficient predators with a sense of humour and the inherited emotional intelligence and energy to have fun.

Sadly, the time for fun and humour for wild dogs is rapidly being curtailed thanks to our greedy misuse of the planet and persisting abuse of predators. As you look at these photographs, remember that those wild dogs surviving in isolated families now find it almost impossible to link up with others. Remember that only perhaps one tenth of the world's population of African wild dogs will ever breed and that every member of their pack is important if they are to do so successfully. To conserve this species requires us to understand its social needs as well as its spatial and feeding requirements, and to make provision.

If ever a book was timely, it is this one. Neil Aldridge's talents as a photographer have captured the spirit and hedonistic nature of this wonderful but long neglected and persecuted carnivore. His selection of images and sensitive narrative of his time at work with them is a huge prompt to us all to appreciate the value of this species. The circle of life is breaking up for African wild dogs and they need our help.

Why should we help? Because they are one of the most beautiful animals you could ever see and the images in this book surely prove this for those of you yet to see an African wild dog and take your own blurred photo. Read this book and know that you must put that experience high on your '100 things to do before you die' list. I guarantee that when you see your first African wild dog, you will do everything you can to ensure that those who come after you will still have that chance. And when you do, Neil's work behind the lens will have achieved its aims.

Introduction

Fifteen years! That's how long it took me to see my first African wild dog in the wild after moving to South Africa in 1991. The pack of dogs was lazing in a patch of burnt bushveld by the side of the road just north of Tshokwane in South Africa's Kruger National Park. When I spotted them I remember cursing myself for only having two shots left on what was my final roll of film but the longer I sat there the more I appreciated the chance to just watch them. This was a rare privilege for most people but especially a wildlife photographer who spends most of his time at such encounters with one eye closed and the other glued to the viewfinder.

By the time of that first unforgettable encounter I was already a qualified field guide and spending a lot of my time in the bush building up my portfolio of wildlife photographs. I knew what I was seeing was special but while you would probably expect me to wheel out the old cliché and say that I was hooked on wild dogs from the moment I saw them, it has been more of a case of my respect and fascination growing the more time that I have spent with these beautiful animals.

It's hard to overlook their perfectly honed hunting design. Huge ears sit like satellite dishes atop a body primed not for fight but for flight, making the African wild dog one of the most efficient carnivores on earth. Yet, it was witnessing the absolute cooperation in a pack of dogs raising a litter of thirteen pups on the banks of the Limpopo River in Botswana that made the strongest impression on me, bringing to mind how much effort these charismatic canids invest in survival.

When I set out to photograph *Underdogs* it was that charisma and survival instinct that I wanted to justify. If I could do that successfully then the reader or anyone viewing these pictures might see why the African wild dog is worth fighting for.

Primed for hunting *(previous spread): Ears like satellite dishes on top of bodies built for endurance...all part of the make up of Africa's most efficient carnivore.*

First impressions *(above): My first encounter with African wild dogs was in South Africa's Kruger National Park in 2005.*

Investing in the future *(opposite): Raising pups is a family affair and this pack in Botswana showed the cooperation that allows wild dogs to raise large litters.*

Land of giants *(overleaf): Baobab trees dominate the landscape of northern South Africa's Limpopo Valley where I spent much of my time following and photographing wild dogs.*

Chasing their tails *(above): African wild dogs trot at a speed of around 10 kilometres per hour, taking them out of tracking range in no time. When the dogs were on the move, we spent a lot of time hiking up to higher ground where the chance of picking up a signal from a radio collar was better.*

Mobile hide *(left): Although usually wary of humans, the pack of wild dogs on South Africa's Venetia Limpopo Nature Reserve were so used to seeing the Land Rover driven by researchers that we were able to get close enough to photograph intimate moments.*

Moonlighting *(opposite): Wild dogs aren't usually nocturnal but they do hunt when the moon is bright, which meant long hours playing catch-up in the dark.*

Showcasing pictures of wild dogs and their pups would only be telling part of the story however. With the continent's wild dog population unstable and with a long history of human-wild dog conflict spilling over into the present day, the species badly needs the efforts of those dedicated few conservationists that work untiringly for their cause. This project always intended to highlight the issues facing the survival of wild dogs and to act as a platform to demonstrate the range of work being done to combat those matters in one of the few remaining regions the African wild dog can call home. For this reason, *Underdogs* took me to a number of locations across Southern Africa. By carefully planning my logistics I hoped to photograph every aspect of African wild dog life and conservation work essential to telling this story.

The wild dogs of the Northern Tuli Game Reserve in eastern Botswana had been part of South Africa's metapopulation but were moved from Marakele National Park in late 2007. The pack raised a large litter of pups in 2008 and I hoped that my timing would be right to witness the emergence of a new litter from their den on the banks of the Limpopo River a year later. In all honesty, I couldn't have timed my arrival in Botswana better and watching 13 one-month old pups exploring their new surroundings under the close eye of a healthy and successful pack still ranks as my most unforgettable wildlife experience.

I had heard that KwaZulu-Natal, South Africa's eastern-most province, was fast becoming the country's wild dog hotspot and the creation of a new pack in the Mkhuze Game Reserve gave me the chance to see this success story for myself. However, my main reason for visiting the region was in fact to witness the community liaison work being undertaken by the Endangered Wildlife Trust (EWT) in communities neighbouring reserves with established wild dog populations.

Venetia Limpopo Nature Reserve near South Africa's borders with Zimbabwe and Botswana was where I spent most of my time. Owned by mining giants De Beers, Venetia Limpopo has been home to a small yet well-researched pack of dogs whose own story echoes many of the trials and tribulations that I hoped

to relate to the survival of the species as a whole. With a focus on research unlike other tourism-centred reserves, I hoped that Venetia would provide me with the opportunity to follow a pack regularly and get to know the dogs and their behaviour.

Even though I had been to the reserve on a recce visit some months earlier and knew that the thick mopane bush would make life difficult for long follows and sequence photography, the first weeks on Venetia Limpopo were almost soul destroying. After seven days and only a fleeting, far-off view I was starting to see my plans of illustrating the lives of these dogs turn into the ochre-red dust of the Limpopo Valley floor.

Day after day, the radio telemetry equipment failed to register a single 'beep' in response to a signal from the radio collars worn by some of the dogs. Had the pack given us the slip? Had they slipped into one of the 'black holes' on the reserve where no signal emanates from? Were they still even on the reserve or, frustratingly, had the telemetry equipment gone on the blink? We scrambled up hills in a bid to get a stronger signal but still nothing. Our morale dropped and our tensions heightened. And, to make matters worse, the brightness of the full moon meant that the dogs would be active by night as well as by day. Each morning they could be tens of kilometres away on the other side of the reserve.

Eventually, dogged perseverance and a slice of luck yielded fresh wild dog tracks in the wet morning sand. With some good old fashioned tracking we soon caught up with the pack in the hills resting off the previous night's meal. From the looks of their heaving stomachs, the prey must have been something close to the size of a kudu. They wouldn't be going anywhere soon after feeding that well and we knew that we now had the chance to slip into their routine. We would rest when they rested and be there before they moved again.

Looking for a needle in a haystack *(right): Locating a pack of African wild dogs requires radio tracking equipment but catching up with them means reading their tracks, knowing the lay of the land, anticipating their next move and plotting a route...all while navigating a Land Rover through rugged terrain. EWT field officer John Power relished that challenge and put me in the right spot time and again.*

Although much of my photography was limited to working from the confines of a vehicle, the wild dogs were accustomed to the Land Rover driven by John Power, EWT's field officer on Venetia. This acceptance of us, coupled with John's ability to manoeuvre a Land Rover in thick mopane bush, meant that the weeks that followed were highly productive.

As we followed alpha female Stellar and her pack it became clear that their day-to-day pattern had become defined by the events of the past. In between hunts, she sought refuge for her pack on rocky high ground in an attempt to avoid running into the lions that had killed her entire litter of pups and her mate the previous year. When we followed the pack on foot where the vehicle could not go, we too hoped that Stellar's judgement was right and that she had learned to avoid lions!

In those first few weeks following the Venetia Limpopo pack I had no idea that the next two years would be such a rollercoaster of events and emotions. When I first saw the pack there were five of them – a large enough pack to regularly hunt prey as large as kudu. At the time of writing this, just one member remains alive. I could try to say that I am glad that three of Stellar's pack were killed by natural enemies instead of at the hands of man. In truth however, with such fragile numbers remaining and with such limited space available to develop suitable habitat, the loss of any adult wild dog of breeding age is a loss to the population as a whole. If I can feel positive about anything, it is that the lives of these dogs may not have been in vain and that by allowing me into their world they have allowed me to inspire you about their magnificent and endangered species.

Enemy of the state *(this spread): Lions are one of the major causes of adult wild dog and pup mortality and decimated the Venetia pack. As a result, keeping tabs on Thikka the lioness and her pride and learning more about lion-wild dog interaction has been a major part of wild dog research on Venetia Limpopo Nature Reserve.*

Honed for Hunting

Africa's painted wolves

Lycaon pictus *(previous spread): The African wild dog's scientific name is a reference to its wolf-like appearance and ancestry and its tricoloured black, white and tan coat.*

Painted dogs *(this spread): The coat pattern of every African wild dog is unique and allows researchers to identify individuals from when they are pups.*

When you first set eyes on an African wild dog trotting through the bush, there is no doubting that what you are looking at is an animal built for hunting. The tricoloured coat pattern blends with the dog's habitat, giving it excellent camouflage. Long limbs carry the animal at a trot at more than ten kilometres an hour with consummate ease. Huge ears pick up every noise keeping them alert to danger and potential prey. But these are not chance characteristics – every element of the African wild dog's anatomy has been honed over time to engineer Africa's most efficient carnivore.

The African wild dog may be a member of the Canidae family but as it's scientific name *Lycaon pictus* suggests, it stands apart from its African neighbours the black-backed jackal and bat-eared fox that the species shares a common ancestor with. The African wild dog is the only member of the genus *Lycaon*, which split from the family tree several million years ago to form a new, unique lineage. The species' genus name *Lycaon* is derived from the Greek for 'wolf', hinting to this common ancestry and the wild dog's wolf-like appearance. Although, as a result of this phylogenetic distinction, the African wild dog cannot interbreed with any of its relatives in the Canidae family. It is a sobering thought that if we keep pushing the species towards extinction, we will be aiding the loss of a genetically unique line within the Canidae family formed millions of years ago.

The wild dog is known by at least three different names in English alone. One of the more common alternatives is the name 'painted dog', which is a more literal reference to the species name *pictus* meaning 'painted' in Latin and refers to the eclectic mix of black, white and tan in the wild dog's coat. As with it's ungulate neighbours the zebra and giraffe, the coat pattern of every African wild dog is unique to each animal. When the pups are born their coats initially lack the tan element. This colour develops after just a few months but the white patches that the pups are born with remain for life. These allow researchers to identify individual dogs from a young age right the way through life. While coat patterns can be very different from one dog to the next, some general characteristics do typify the species – the long white tip of the tail, dark ears and a jet-black muzzle.

Like a long distance runner, the African wild dog is efficiently light with long, thin legs. Adults typically stand 70 centimetres tall at the shoulder and rarely weigh more than 30 kilograms. Although, further north in what remains of their natural range, individuals are generally smaller, weighing between six and ten kilograms less than their cousins in Southern Africa. There are theories that this variation is connected to the size of the prey species favoured in the respective regions, yet the predominant factor in the determination of prey and in the success of hunting is pack size.

The African wild dog is an extremely social predator and lives in packs as small as two and as large as 30 individuals. Pack members rarely spend much time away from each other and nearly every activity plays a part in cementing social bonds and hierarchy. Each pack has a dominant pair and this alpha male and alpha female have the sole breeding rights within the unit. The pair will often lead the pack when hunting too.

The typical wild dog hunt is preceded by a boisterous rally. This social act incorporates plenty of physical goading and noisy yittering and squealing and is often repeated until all dogs are ready and prepared for hunting. Once rallied, the pack sets out into the early morning or late afternoon light in search of their quarry. Wild dogs are crepuscular, meaning that they are more active in the hours around dawn and dusk and are less likely to run into competition from other marauding predators like lions and hyenas when hunting in this way.

Relying on good eyesight, wild dogs spot their prey and then give chase. Sometimes herds of larger animals will stand their ground in a bid to defend themselves against the excited pack but prey in smaller numbers flee for their lives, often resulting in a lengthy chase. Owing to their stamina, wild dogs do not rely as much on ambush hunting strategies, unlike other carnivores. Instead, the pack fans out to flank any sideways movements by the chosen quarry and pursues at speed. With a top speed of 60 kilometres per hour, hunting dogs can often be out-run initially but over a distance of several kilometres the exhausted prey is run down.

Determined hunter *(opposite): The wild dog is Africa's most efficient carnivore, helped by its physical attributes and social nature.*

Kinship personified *(above): Almost every activity in wild dog society plays a part in cementing bonds and hierarchies, from boisterous pre-hunt rallying to cooperative feeding.*

Casual drinkers *(this spread): By feeding quickly and possessing long large intestines, wild dogs absorb a lot of vital fluids from their prey. As a result, they can go for long periods without drinking when they need to. When water is plentiful however, they will bathe and play in it with great relish.*

It is well documented that despite their immense speed, cheetahs can only sustain a chase for a short distance before their bodies overheat. This problem does not afflict African wild dogs as they are adapted to deal with the heat stress associated with running at speed over long distances. During these long chases wild dogs repeatedly try to bite the flanks of their prey. This is as a result of another key difference between the African wild dog and the cheetah. Wild dogs lack the razor-sharp dewclaw that cheetahs use to trip their prey once they are close enough. Instead, once one dog is close enough to bite and has a hold, the rest of the pack converges to stop the prey in its tracks and it is quickly disembowelled.

Just as cooperative hunting accounts for a greater success rate and allows a pack to bring down prey much larger than the weight and size of a single wild dog, so cooperative feeding helps to consume prey quickly. Wild dogs have an exceptionally strong bite for their size and possess an arsenal of teeth that has evolved solely for a predatory lifestyle. Large premolars and shearing lower carnassials rip through bone and flesh and so once a pack begins what looks like a messy game of tug-of-war with their prey, limbs are torn away from each other quickly and devoured in an instant.

This way of feeding may seem vicious and it has drawn scorn from many, including hunters and conservationists alike, but it is the result of design. Being relatively lightweight, wild dogs need to eat quickly to avoid detection and confrontation with other predators. Hyenas have been known to follow packs on the hunt while lions never need a second invitation to challenge wild dogs for their meal. Only sometimes does the advantage of sheer numbers over a solitary aggressor mean that a pack can defend their kill.

One other physical attribute that allows wild dogs to eat large amounts of food quickly is also one of their most valuable

***Fast food** (this page): Large razor-like teeth, an exceptionally strong bite and a distensible stomach mean that wild dogs tend to make short work of prey.*

***Opportunists extraordinaire** (right): Both brown and spotted hyena represent the ever-present threat of marauding scavengers and are known to follow wild dog packs in the hope of wrestling a free meal.*

Dinner time *(above): At just a few weeks old wild dog pups begin to eat meat that is carried back to the den in the stomachs of the hunters and then regurgitated on request.*

A bundle of hope *(right): A one month old wild dog pup explores the world outside its den on the banks of the mighty Limpopo River. Pups are born black and white and only develop the tan colour in their coat after a few months.*

tools for successful reproduction. Having a distensible stomach means that wild dogs can consume their prey in a very short time. Ordinarily this would allow the pack to retire to a shady spot to sleep off a meal, safe in the knowledge that the entire animal had been eaten and that no telltale bones or organs had been left to attract scavengers. When a pack dens and is raising pups however, the hunters will carry food back in their bloated stomachs and regurgitate meat to feed the pups, the alpha female and any other adult babysitters not on the hunt.

The tiny pups start to eat meat after just three or four weeks, by which time they start to spend time outside of the den. The regurgitation of meat is solicited amidst a frenzy of excited high-pitched yittering and is stimulated by the licking of the muzzles of the dogs returning from the hunt. Adult wild dogs have to work hard to find enough food to feed themselves and an entire litter of voracious pups.

The average litter size is around 11 pups but anywhere up to 20 can be born after the usual gestation period of ten weeks. With so many mouths to feed and so many threats to the survival of the litter in the form of predation and disease, only around 50 per cent of pups survive their first year. There is a general correlation though between pack size and pup survival, with larger packs ensuring a higher rate of reproductive success. This is mainly down to the inherent sense of responsibility that the hard working adult wild dogs have towards the pack as a whole. Those pups that are lucky enough to be born into a large pack enjoy the luxury of having a mother and extra babysitters to look after them while a team of hunters provide an almost constant supply of food.

As much as the alpha pair attempts to suppress courtship in subordinate adults, occasionally another female will give birth. When this happens it is very much a lottery as to whether the alpha female will adopt the pups as her own, help with the care and upbringing of them or simply kill them. It is believed that whether she feels the pack can provide enough food for all of the pups or not may have an influence on her judgement. Despite this enforcement of dominance from the alpha female, some

alpha females have been proven through DNA testing to have mated with more than one male during oestrus and produced litters of multiple paternity. This does not have an impact on the care given to the litter by the pack however, especially as alpha males take no greater part in caring for the pups than the other adults in the pack.

Alpha females often utilise old aardvark burrows for a den and may use the same site year after year. However, wild dog packs have huge home ranges, regularly in excess of 100,000 hectares, and the pack will leave the den once the pups are about three months old to return to a more roaming existence. By this time the pups are fully weaned and, through their time playing and honing skills outside the den, are able to move with the pack. The energy from every hunt and the care from every individual given to the pups leads up to this moment, yet they remain in mortal danger as so few reach even a year old.

Of those that do reach a year old, some soon disperse in same sex groups, leaving their natal home range in search of a group from the opposite sex that have similarly broken away from another pack. Although this step potentially weakens their natal pack in the short term, it gives young subordinate dogs the opportunity to form a new pack and to reproduce. While searching for new mates and their own suitable home range, dispersers can travel hundreds of kilometres. By carrying their genes such distances, these young trailblazers are ensuring the genetic diversity of the species. Yet the threat to genetic integrity is a problem that faces endangered species worldwide and with so many fragmented populations of African wild dogs cut off from one another by human development, how to maintain that integrity naturally is the greatest challenge facing wild dog conservation.

The power of the pack *(left): Every member of a wild dog pack has an inherent responsibility in caring for or providing for the alpha female's large litter.*

Predator in the making *(overleaf): This pup may be taking the vegetarian option for now but every activity around the den hones the predatory skills of the next generation of hunters.*

Fragmented Freedom

the metapopulation concept

With little more than 3,000 individuals living in the wild, the African wild dog is without doubt one of the world's most endangered carnivores, perhaps even scarcer than that great icon of endangered wildlife, the tiger. Equally alarming is the reality that wild dog numbers are still decreasing. Although wild dogs range over huge distances and can turn up unexpectedly in areas where they may not have been seen for decades, it is generally regarded that the species has been eradicated from 25 of the 39 countries that formed its historical range. The wild dog now clings to existence in pockets of southern and east Africa.

With human development encroaching on natural habitat and with wild dog packs requiring large territories, these pockets of existence are rarely enough to ensure a population can exist in a sustainable way. As dispersal routes between packs become cut off by a succession of fences, roads and unsuitable habitat, so competition with other predators and the threat of genetically restricted populations intensifies. However, in the late 1990s an approach was drafted to combat the threats to the conservation of the wild dog in South Africa. The notion involved identifying locations suitable for the management of isolated populations of wild dogs. These individual populations would then be managed as a single metapopulation to complement the country's only conservation area large enough to sustain a genetically viable wild dog population – the renowned Kruger National Park. This new approach would see individual animals or small single-sex groups physically translocated periodically between protected areas to form new breeding packs, thereby mimicking the wild dog's natural dispersal behaviour and ensuring genetic diversity is maintained. This concept was not developed as a permanent solution to the conservation of the species but something had to be done to arrest the decline in numbers and buy conservation bodies more time. With South Africa's fragmented landscape of game farms and private reserves, the metapopulation project seemed a logical fit.

Diseases like rabies and canine distemper have severely affected wild dog populations elsewhere in Africa. Outbreaks of disease tend to be swift, aided by the wild dog's own highly sociable nature. The huge Serengeti-Mara ecosystem spanning Kenya and Tanzania had lost all of its wild dogs to disease by the end of 1991. If a similar catastrophic decline or even a local extinction were to afflict the wild dogs of South Africa's Kruger National Park, the metapopulation could feasibly ensure that a managed and intensively researched population could be utilised for any reintroduction into the flagship park.

Adapting to their surroundings *(previous spread): A member of the Venetia Limpopo pack stops to contemplate a distant quarry. Wild dogs living in these smaller, isolated game reserves have learned to use fences to their advantage when hunting.*

Safety net *(this spread): The sociable nature of wild dogs ensures that outbreaks of diseases like rabies spread rapidly. If an outbreak was to afflict the Kruger National Park's wild dogs, the metapopulation could provide a genetically healthy pool of dogs for a reintroduction.*

On borrowed time? *(following spread): More needs to be done to understand the problems facing the species in South Africa's Kruger National Park, especially north of the Shingwedzi River where the park is open to Mozambique and will soon be open to Zimbabwe. The declining wild dog numbers in this world-renowned conservation area reflect the population trend across the African continent.*

The Distribution of the African Wild Dog

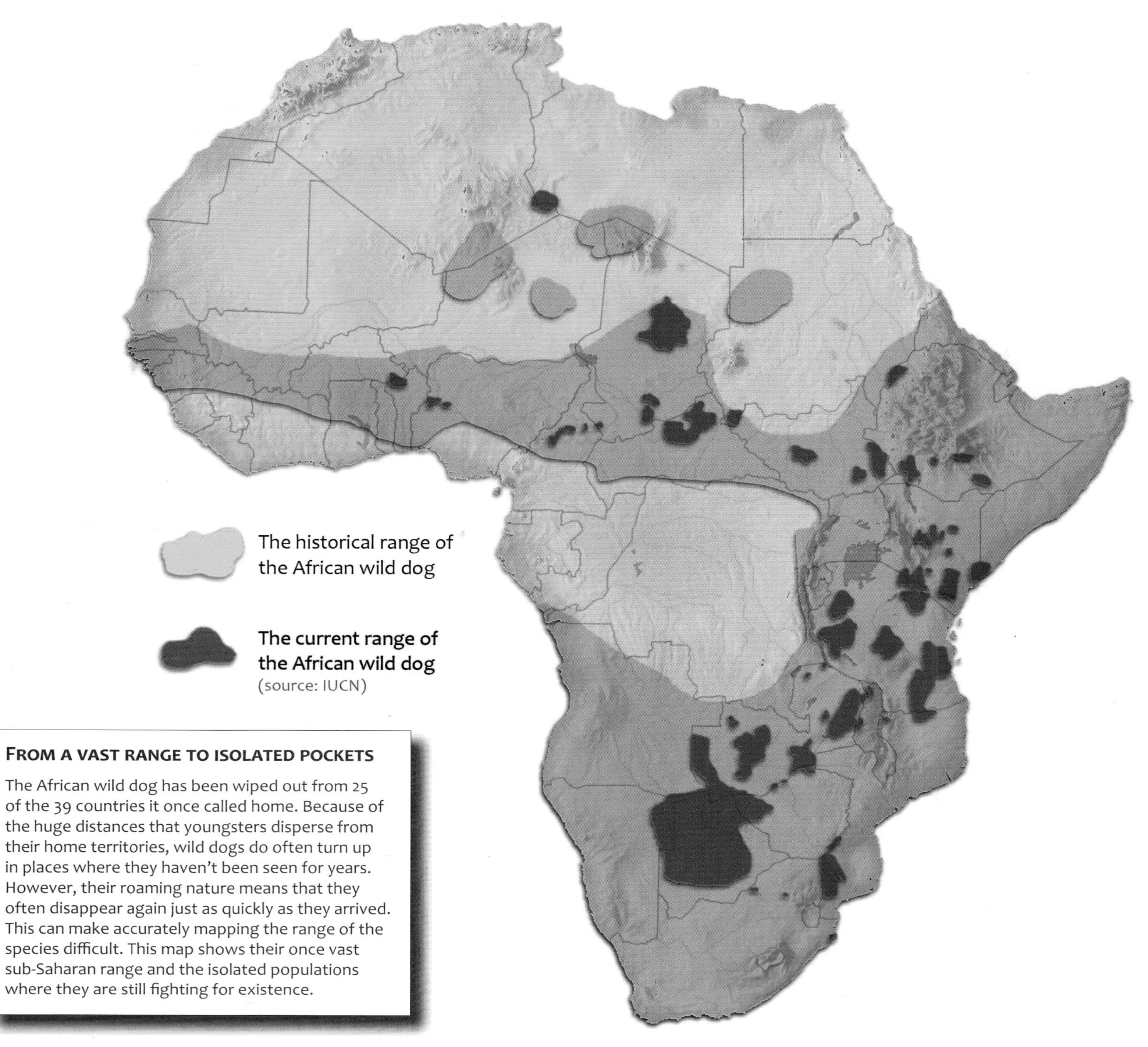

FROM A VAST RANGE TO ISOLATED POCKETS

The African wild dog has been wiped out from 25 of the 39 countries it once called home. Because of the huge distances that youngsters disperse from their home territories, wild dogs do often turn up in places where they haven't been seen for years. However, their roaming nature means that they often disappear again just as quickly as they arrived. This can make accurately mapping the range of the species difficult. This map shows their once vast sub-Saharan range and the isolated populations where they are still fighting for existence.

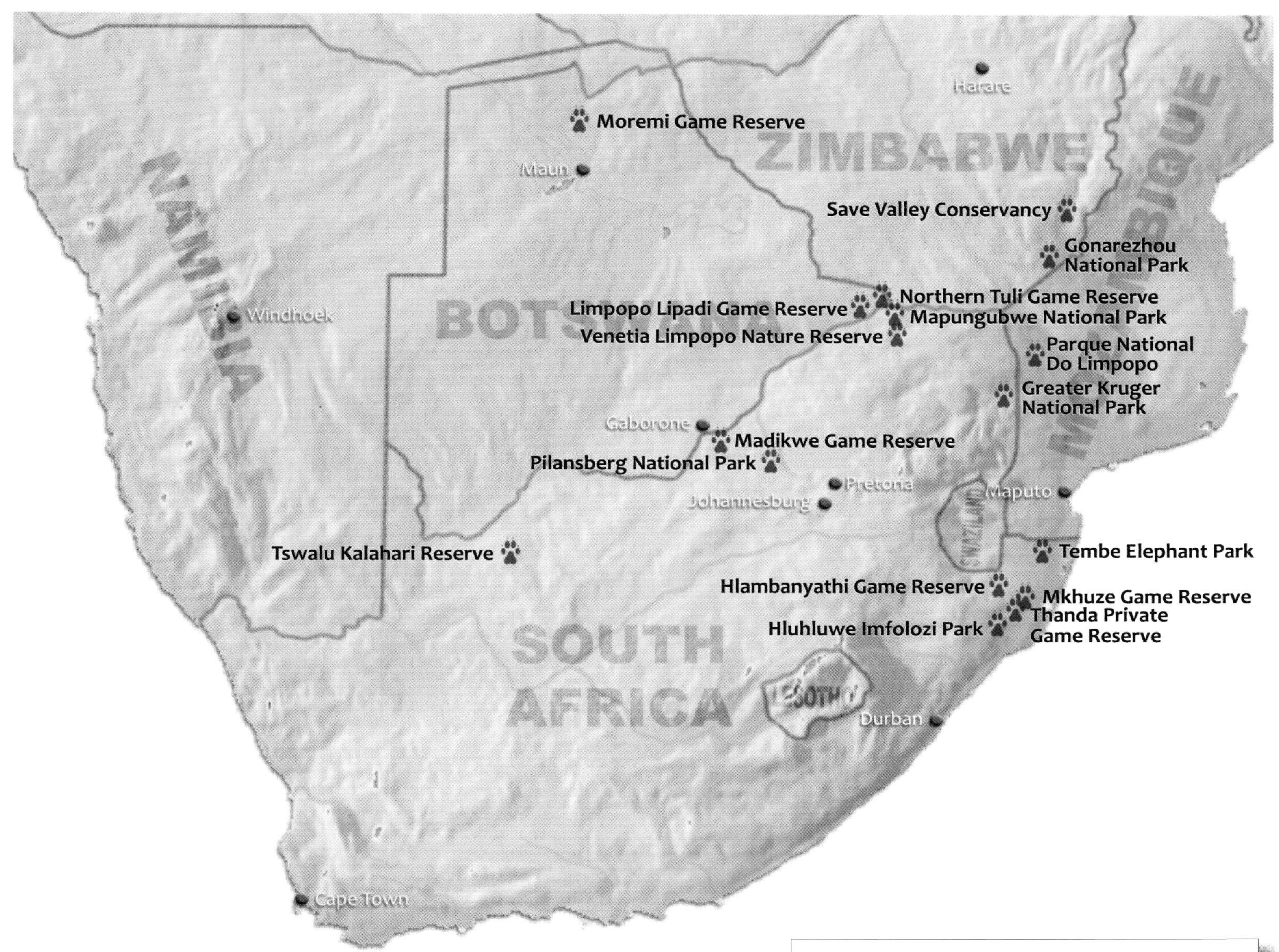

SIGNIFICANT SITES IN SOUTHERN AFRICA

This map shows those national parks and game reserves that are crucial to telling the story of South Africa's wild dogs. These sites are either home to significant wild dog populations or they have played a part in the success of the metapopulation since its inception in the late 1990's. South Africa's Greater Kruger National Park and Botswana's Moremi Game Reserve are regarded as Southern Africa's only two truly genetically viable wild dog populations.

Although generations of visitors to South Africa's flagship national park have enjoyed memorable yet fleeting views of these elusive carnivores, recent census figures have shown a steady decline in the Kruger Park's wild dog numbers. This has lead to calls for a greater understanding of the population there, especially in the northern regions of the park where little is known about the packs living there and where fences have been removed to link Kruger with neighbouring Mozambique's Limpopo National Park. The timing of new research would also be significant ahead of plans to extend the conservation area into Zimbabwe to include the Gonarezhou National Park.

When the metapopulation was established it consisted of wild dog packs in only two locations – the Hluhluwe Imfolozi Park in KwaZulu-Natal and the Madikwe Game Reserve in North West Province – after which it grew to include up to a dozen sites. With such a fragile number of wild dogs spread thinly across the various isolated sub-populations though, the success of any pack or the formation of a new one could never be guaranteed. The implementation of the metapopulation project did succeed in identifying and securing wild dog habitat and in providing a basis for much needed research. Yet, to stabilise the nation's declining wild dog population and to form new packs on suitable reserves, new dogs needed to be introduced from somewhere. With research indicating that smaller packs stand less chance of successfully reproducing in the wild than larger ones, removing adult wild dogs solely from existing packs and diminishing their chances of survival was not the answer.

In 1995, three captive-bred female wild dogs from Ann Van Dyk's De Wildt Cheetah Centre were released into an enclosure at Madikwe Game Reserve with a group of wild males brought from the Kruger National Park. The pack bonded successfully, defying the belief of many in the conservation fraternity at the time, and were released onto the reserve. This successful and groundbreaking trial laid the foundation for the formation of new packs on protected land to enhance the metapopulation. Since that first successful reintroduction using captive-bred wild dogs, the experiment has been successfully repeated several times on a number of reserves across South Africa.

Something to smile about *(this spread): The Hluhluwe Imfolozi Park was one of South Africa's first metapopulation sites. Since then, the success of the park's wild dog population has been a comparative anomaly among declining national numbers.*

New beginnings *(this spread): A babysitter rests nearby while tiny pups explore the world outside their den. This pack was relocated to Botswana from South Africa in 2007 after repeatedly breaking out into hostile territory neighbouring their home in Marakele National Park. Not all trespassing packs are this lucky.*

After the Kruger National Park, the KwaZulu-Natal province represents South Africa's most stable and genetically viable population of wild dogs. Having earned a reputation in the conservation world for its role in saving the southern white rhino from extinction in the 1900s, the region's main reserve, the Hluhluwe Imfolozi Park, has experienced something of a wild dog boom. This is good news in its own right yet it also comes at an important time as numbers in the Kruger National Park continue to be of concern.

KwaZulu-Natal is one area of the country where an increase in land available to wild dog conservation has allowed for the introduction of new packs using a blend of wild and captive-reared animals. Private game reserves and larger provincial parks alike have committed to providing valuable territory for a predator in dire need of space. To capitalise on this commitment, single sex groups of captive-bred wild dogs were introduced in 2009 and 2010 from De Wildt on to KwaZulu-Natal's Mkhuze Game Reserve to be bonded with small groups from the wild.

The reintroduction of wild dogs into an area is not always a simple result of pull factors. All too often, packs of wild dogs are removed from unsuitable habitat or land where they are made ruthlessly unwelcome and new, suitable territory must be found quickly. In some cases, vets and wildlife authorities are only able to save the defenceless pups after the killing of the adults at the hands of the landowner. With no pack to guide the pups and teach them how to survive in the wild, these youngsters often face a captive existence. Thankfully, the trials carried out with the reintroduction of captive-bred De Wildt wild dogs opened the door for these wild-born, captive-reared pups to eventually return to a life in the wild and in 2010 a group of four captive-reared male dogs were translocated from Botswana to Mkhuze in KwaZulu-Natal to be bonded with two females from the wild.

Possibly the most successful translocation of wild dogs from a hostile situation to new beginnings occurred in November 2007. A pack of 18 wild dogs was moved from South Africa's Marakele National Park to Botswana's Northern Tuli Game Reserve after the pack had consistently broken through fences onto neighbouring farmland. Faced with the very real chance of losing the pack for good to persecution or disease outside the safety of Marakele's boundaries, the decision was made to find the pack a new home. After being held for six months in a holding facility known as a boma, the pack was released into the unfenced Tuli wilderness in April 2008.

A captive solution *(left): Captive-bred wild dogs were bonded with wild-living dogs and released onto Madikwe Game Reserve in 1995. This experiment paved the way for further successful introductions of captive-bred dogs into the metapopulation, such as this male and his three brothers onto Mkhuze Game Reserve in KwaZulu-Natal in 2009.*

Born to be wild *(this page): Wild-born pups are often saved and taken in to be reared in captivity after adult members of their pack have been killed by humans. This used to mean a life in captivity but the identification of new, suitable locations has allowed new packs to be created under the metapopulation using reintroduced wild-born dogs.*

The darting process *(this spread): After hours of waiting, a vet finally gets a clear shot and fires a tranquilliser dart towards his target. Minutes later, the drug has taken effect and the young wild dog can be approached and the dart removed.*

Translocation *(overleaf): A team of vets and researchers move quickly to treat the dart wounds and prepare the young male wild dog for the long journey ahead.*

RHINO
FRIEND

Precious cargo *(this spread): Researchers remove a radio collar from a tranquillised young male African wild dog before dousing him with water to keep him cool. He is then loaded into a crate for the 900 kilometre journey to his new home where it is hoped he will establish a new breeding pack.*

Following a translocation, a group of wild dogs are usually held in bomas for some time while they are allowed to acclimatise to their new surroundings. If two groups are to be bonded, the behaviour and reaction of the groups towards one another along a fenced partition is usually observed first before the partition is removed. Although it is never ideal to keep a pack contained for long periods, time in the boma allows for bonding and for hierarchies to be established within the group. This in turn helps the pack function as a more organised unit when hunting and surviving out in the wild.

The success of the metapopulation project relies heavily on bomas, not just as holding facilities but also as vital research resources. For vets and researchers, the confines of the boma allows for identification photographs to be taken of every animal's individual markings to aid quick recognition in the field after their release. Darting and immobilising such nervous and energetic creatures is also made easier by the restrictions of the enclosure. Following a darting, vital genetic information can be collected from each dog and added to a national database that serves to sustain the genetic integrity of the population. State veterinary health checks can also be performed before any cross-border movements and, if necessary, radio collars can be fitted so that researchers can keep tabs on the whereabouts of the dogs after they have been released from the boma.

Tourists often remark at how unsightly a radio collar can be on an animal and wildlife photographers tend to avoid collared animals at almost all costs in the mindset that the animal is somehow less wild. However, these neckpieces are absolutely vital pieces of equipment for researchers working to conserve one of the world's most endangered carnivores. With a pack of wild dogs roaming a huge territory at a speed in excess of ten kilometres per hour at a mere trot, tracking without the help of these transmitting devices would be futile and the fuel costs and time incurred would be excessive.

The introduction of GPS collars has not only further increased tracking efficiency but it has vastly advanced our knowledge about the movement patterns of African wild dogs. The collars

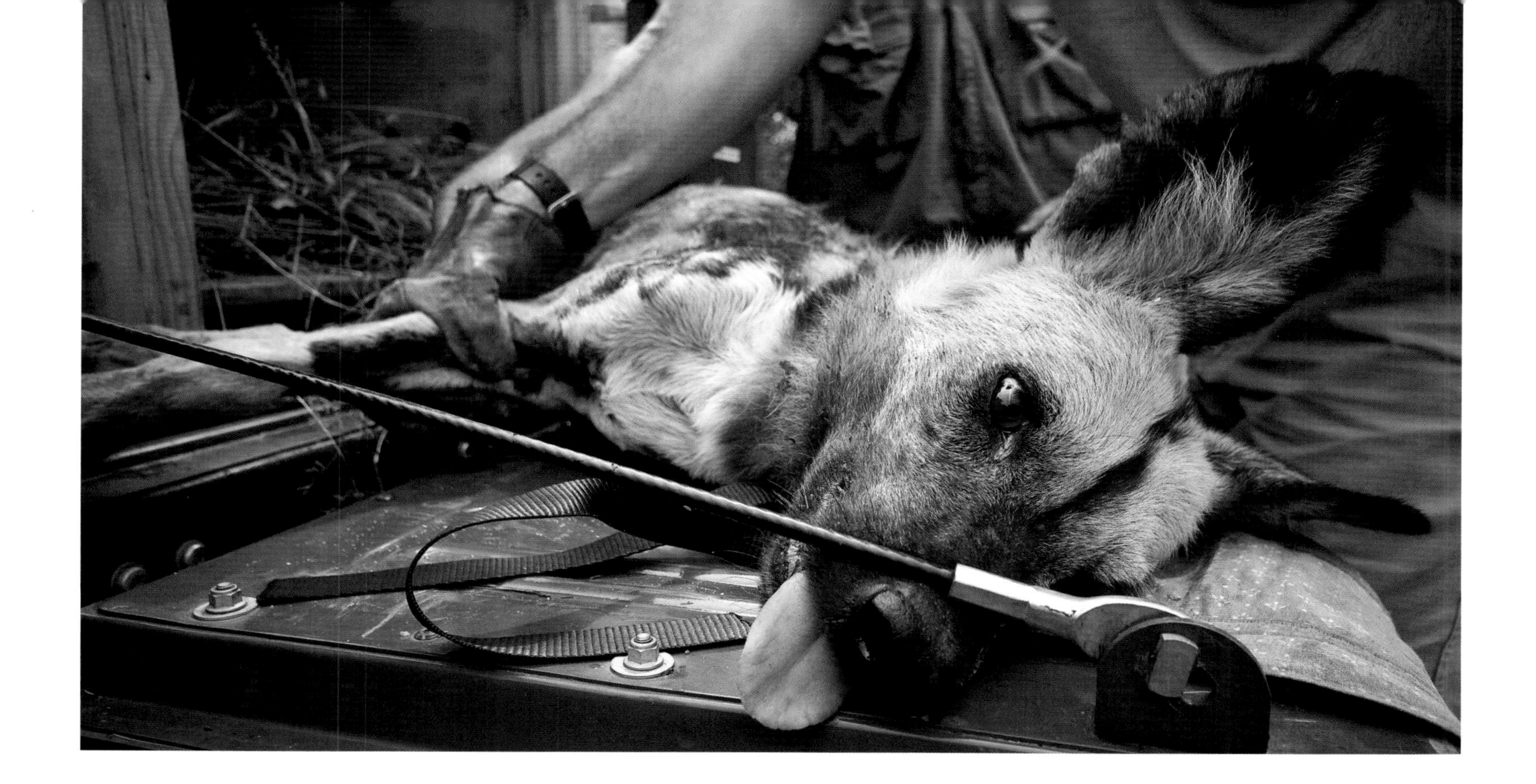

relay GPS coordinates of the whereabouts of the animal via the cellular phone network. The results gathered from GPS collars fitted to wild dogs from KwaZulu-Natal's Hluhluwe Imfolozi Park has staggered researchers, showing groups dispersing hundreds of kilometres to find new territories and to form new packs. This invaluable information has helped South Africa's Wild Dog Advisory Group and the Endangered Wildlife Trust take the metapopulation process forward.

The management-intensive metapopulation project was never meant to serve as a long-term, definitive solution to stemming the collapse of African wild dog numbers in South Africa and rebuilding the population. Its aim of identifying new, suitable habitat for wild dogs on safe and appropriately-sized reserves is being met. What the feedback received from GPS collars can highlight is the exact areas outside of protected reserves that wild dogs are dispersing into. This information can help researchers liaise with landowners and communities in the regions next to

reserves to ensure safe passages for dispersing groups of wild dogs. If safe buffer zones and dispersal corridors can be set up then natural movements can be encouraged over the current method of immobilisation and physical translocation. The costs associated with physical translocation and the stress put on dogs during the process would also be minimised.

It is not only community leaders and landowners that need to be won over in the battle to forge a future for the African wild dog however. There remain many game farm managers that are indifferent towards wild dogs. If detractors can be convinced of the tourism and conservation benefits of hosting resident packs of wild dogs then the metapopulation network can be expanded. In turn, fences between neighbouring game reserves could be removed and the landscape-scale, cross-border conservation efforts that are in place elsewhere in Africa could be applied. It is this joined-up, collaborative and neighbour-friendly approach to conservation that the wide-roaming African wild dog needs if it is to survive and flourish.

In essence, although the forward-thinking efforts of the Wild Dog Advisory Group and its conservation partners are helping to piece together the different parts of the spatial jigsaw, there is an ever-diminishing niche for predators in a rapidly developing continent. As a result, there is always likely to be an element of human intervention in the management of *Lycaon pictus*. We have pushed the species to the margins of existence that it is no longer plausible to turn a blind eye and let the few remaining wild dogs living in splintered populations simply live out their destiny. Fortunately, there are those few who, all too often for scant reward, are prepared to dedicate their efforts to giving a fighting chance to a much overlooked and uncelebrated species.

***Radio tracking** (right): Packs of African wild dogs roam such huge territories and move so quickly that tracking without the help of radio telemetry devices would be futile and the time and fuel costs incurred would be excessive.*

***Necessary neckwear** (overleaf): A member of the Venetia Limpopo pack sports a radio collar. The collars are vital tools for research and are designed not to hinder movement.*

By the Barrel of a Gun

life and death in the African bush

Nothing wasted *(previous spread): African wild dogs are voracious feeders. This adult wild dog won't waste a morsal and will then help to feed pups and other adults back at the den by regurgitating food.*

Paintings from the past *(above): Archaeologist Tim Forssman interprets one of the Limpopo Valley's many Bushman rock art sites painted during man's respectful existence alongside Africa's wildlife.*

Wild dogs, Jackals or Mongooses? *(opposite): This row of animals on a fantastically rich rock art panel on the Machete farm in the Limpopo Valley has been interpreted by some archaeologists as a pack of African wild dogs. A handful of detailed Bushman paintings like this one show the mythological significance of the wild dog to the traditional Bushmen of Southern Africa.*

Across the continent of Africa, the existence of the African wild dog as a species is inextricably linked to an invention that has shaped the modern world – the gun. Nowadays, researchers rely on its dart-projecting ability to immobilise animals for fitting radio collars and for translocation but it hasn't always been this way. Wild dogs have fared badly since big game hunters arrived in Africa in their droves from the end of the 1800s. It was the hunting technique of these super efficient carnivores that led many influential hunters and early game wardens to label them as cruel and murderous and to call for the wild dog's widespread extermination. The sentiments of British big game hunter R.C.F. Maughan that the species was an 'abomination' and a 'blot upon the many interesting wild things' sum up the feelings of the time. And so the arrival of the colonial superpowers in Africa marked the beginning of the end of man's respectful existence in nature alongside Africa's wild creatures.

Before the aggressive European colonisation of land inhabited by Bushman hunter-gatherer communities, during a time when the African air was filled with the sounds of traditional singing instead of the crack of gunfire, the African wild dog was revered for its flawless hunting abilities, the very quality that drew scorn from Africa's brash new settlers. Sadly, there are few traditional Bushman communities remaining, although their descendants and their wonderfully detailed rock art allow us to understand a relationship between man and beast all but lost with the arrival of the great white hunter.

Various parts of an African wild dog's body are believed to have spiritual, medicinal and physical importance in some traditional African communities. Perhaps most notably, Bushmen across Southern Africa are known to have eaten the heart of the wild dog in a bid to become more adept hunters with the courage, cooperation and swiftness of the animal. Other specific uses are less clear however, such as the use of wild dog bones by Bushmen as tobacco pipes. Of course, nowadays it is difficult to understand how these uses infer any form of respect when they necessitate the killing of a wild dog. Yet, following a kill, almost every body part of a wild dog would be utilised in some useful way in stark contrast to the way carcasses were left by

colonial hunters to rot in the African sun after falling under a hail of bullets. The traditional usage of wild dog body parts still occurs in parts of Southern Africa today but, thankfully, of the dozens of recorded traditional uses of these parts, not all are consumptive and require the killing of an animal. In areas of Zimbabwe, for example, wild dog faeces is collected for it is believed to cure those suffering from dizziness and it is used to treat tetanus.

The importance of the wild dog to traditional communities goes far beyond physical practices. The interpretation of Bushman rock art across Southern Africa allows us to understand the mythological and religious beliefs Bushmen associated with the species. Because Bushmen are believed to have only painted those animals that had symbolic relevance, the appearance of wild dogs in rock art panels across Southern Africa hints to their important role in Bushman mythology. Irregularities in body size and proportions, as well as the physical effects of hundreds

A tall order *(above): Felling a male kudu like this represents a real challenge for wild dogs. The bite marks on the flanks tell of an epic struggle during a long chase. However, it was the hyenas that won the spoils on this occasion.*

Relentless hunters *(right): With long limbs and a large heart, wild dogs are built for endurance. They often chase prey to the point where it can no longer continue and collapses through exhaustion before being disembowelled. This hunting technique earned wild dogs the scorn of big game hunters arriving in Africa to plunder its wild riches.*

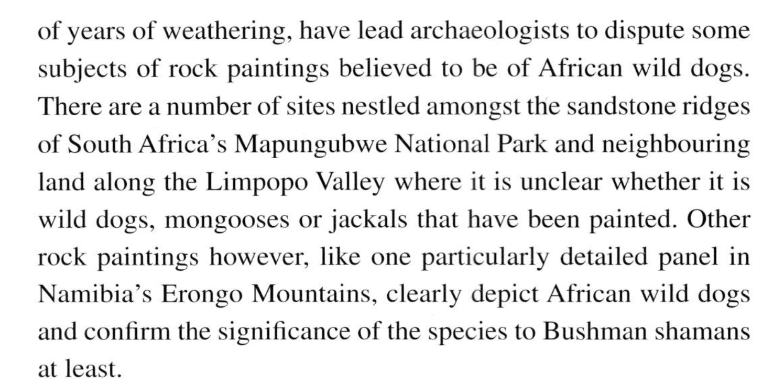

of years of weathering, have lead archaeologists to dispute some subjects of rock paintings believed to be of African wild dogs. There are a number of sites nestled amongst the sandstone ridges of South Africa's Mapungubwe National Park and neighbouring land along the Limpopo Valley where it is unclear whether it is wild dogs, mongooses or jackals that have been painted. Other rock paintings however, like one particularly detailed panel in Namibia's Erongo Mountains, clearly depict African wild dogs and confirm the significance of the species to Bushman shamans at least.

It is believed that it was the shamans in Bushman society who were responsible for adorning caves and rocks with detailed paintings of sacred animals using feathers, their fingers or basic brushes. These rocks acted not just as canvasses for shamans but as a partition between the spirit world and this world. In these paintings they would make use of carnivores like lions and, to a lesser extent, wild dogs as metaphors for threatening or unknown forces entering their landscape. While practices in rock painting disappeared among Bushman culture around the time of the Anglo-Boer War at the turn of the 20th century, a small number of shamans continue to employ trance dances to this day as a way of entering the spirit world and carrying out healing. While in an altered state of consciousness brought about by hours of rhythmic dancing, shamans take on the senses and forms of animals and enter the spirit world. Being the most widely revered of all the animals in Bushman mythology, the eland is more commonly embodied than any other animal. To make themselves appear fiercer or braver when tackling disease or adversity however, it is believed that shamans sometimes take on the forms of carnivores when they enter the spirit world to face the spirits.

In some Bushman communities, Shamans are known to have sometimes worn the skins of African wild dogs and it is a belief that some can take on the form and qualities of Africa's most efficient predator before setting out to hunt. It is no surprise that Bushmen have identified with the African wild dog and sought to capture and employ their powers of stamina and bravery. Like Bushmen, wild dogs head out to hunt in groups and return with

food to feed their family. While Bushmen are known to still set traps for certain prey species, they share a vital characteristic with wild dogs in their prodigious and unflinching stamina when hunting, allowing them to tire their prey before dispatching it.

Being a pack hunter and having the physiology for prolonged chases, wild dogs usually run down their prey to the point of exhaustion before swiftly disembowelling it and consuming it in its entirety in a matter of minutes. This method relies heavily on the hunting pack maintaining a good visual of their quarry and is one reason why wild dogs hunt predominantly during daylight hours, only choosing to risk running into their nocturnal enemies on bright, moonlit nights.

Although perhaps gruesome to many people's eyes, the wild dog's technique of dispatch can be much swifter than that of gradual strangulation used by lions and leopards, and is surely less heart-wrenching for most than watching cheetahs play with a helpless young gazelle for hours. Yet, the wild dog's label of inhumanity has contributed hugely to the species' widespread decline. By immediately devouring their prey, wild dogs take in valuable fluids from vital organs, allowing them to live largely independently from fresh water. This speedy consumption has another significant survival benefit in that it diminishes the chance of having their hunting activity noticed by marauding scavengers. Vultures are quick to spot kills and their presence can attract jackals, hyenas and even lions.

Across most of Southern Africa, the abundant impala makes up around two thirds of a wild dog's diet yet in northern Botswana's Moremi Game Reserve, this figure rises to a staggering 85 per cent. Further north on the open plains of Kenya and Tanzania, the similarly-sized Thomson's gazelle replaces the impala as the prey of choice. In a straight chase, both the impala and gazelle reach speeds marginally quicker than that of a wild dog, often allowing the hunted to indulge in a series of elaborate leaps known as pronking to show off to their pursuers how fit and strong they are as individuals. This sign of vitality and strength will sometimes make the hunters turn their attention to weaker animals. Wild dogs do possess greater stamina however and by continuing the chase and working together they are successful in eight out of ten hunts.

Indefatigable stamina and teamwork allow wild dogs to fell prey much larger than impala and Thomson's gazelle however. With many mouths to feed, especially when denning and raising their characteristically large litters, these are handy hunting traits. Yet, on smaller reserves where boundaries are fortified with game fences to keep predators from crossing onto neighbouring land, wild dog packs employ a cunning hunting technique that shows how intelligence and ability to learn has helped members of the Canidae family to conquer almost every habitat on the planet. It is precisely these fences, designed to restrict and contain them, that wild dogs have learned to use in their favour. Prey animals of all sizes from diminutive steenboks up to large kudu bulls are chased and shepherded towards the cordon where the blind panic of the hunt often sees the victim collide with the wires, giving the pursuing hunters their chance to move in for the kill. This technique is not infallible however and prey regularly slip through or jump over the wires.

Packs living in East Africa are generally known to contain more members than those living on many of South Africa's reserves, further increasing their ability to prey on larger animals like wildebeest and kudu. In Tanzania's vast Serengeti National Park and Selous Game Reserve, wildebeest were recorded as the second most favoured prey species of wild dogs. Despite their broad distribution and relative abundance, plains zebra on the

***Making hay while the sun shines** (this spread): African wild dogs are more active during the hours around dawn and dusk. Hunting at this time makes them less likely to encounter their nocturnal mortal nemeses, lions. Only when the moon is bright and near full will they break this pattern and take their chances.*

other hand represent a more formidable challenge. Sharp hooves on the end of a vicious kick have been known to seriously injure lions. For a lightweight predator like a wild dog, a kick from a zebra could be fatal and so it is little wonder that other species are preferred. Similarly, the sharp tusks of the hardy warthog have inflicted serious wounds in defence against hunting wild dogs. It was a tusk through the lower jaw that lead to the death of the 11-year-old alpha male of the Venetia Limpopo wild dog pack in 2006.

Showing a preference for kudu and impala does the wild dog no favours with the professional hunting industry however. Both of these antelope (the kudu in particular) are prized trophies for big game hunters. With the protected wild dog holding no commercial value, an efficient predator residing on commercial hunting property can become a serious economic headache for landowners. Unfortunately, wild dogs do not always fare more favourably in the minds of game reserve managers either. The 'Big Five' has become a big brand that has made an African safari a must-do for holiday makers. Yet, on some reserves, the success of the Big Five has come at a cost for other species like the wild dog that are less popular. With paying guests flying in from all corners of the globe to see Africa's big cats, many game reserve managers would be more inclined to sustain their lion and leopard populations over housing a population of wild dogs. After all, keeping a game reserve well stocked with prey species like impala and kudu costs money but if the predators feeding on that prey are generating tourism then the predator-prey balance becomes financially viable. If guests are not interested in seeing wild dogs, the species becomes uneconomic for landowners and in this age of commercialism, that which has no value is rarely endured. Sadly, the expansion (and therefore the success) of the wild dog metapopulation in South Africa has been at the mercy of such issues as some managers of suitable game reserves have time and again shown a disinclination to welcome wild dogs and play a crucial part in securing the future of the species in their country.

***Dog food** (left): Beautiful and plentiful, the impala is the preferred prey of African wild dogs across much of the predator's remaining range, making up two thirds of their diet in Southern Africa and up to 85 per cent of their food in Moremi, Botswana.*

Worthy adversaries *(this spread): Large packs of wild dogs have been known to hunt zebra in East Africa but the kick of this equine demands respect. Similarly, the tusks of the plucky warthog have brought about the end of many wild dogs during frenzied hunts, including the 11-year-old alpha male of the Venetia Limpopo pack in 2006.*

Fence patrol *(previous spread): The Venetia Limpopo pack moves along the reserve's western fenceline. Being a relatively small pack, these wild dogs learned to make use of the reserve's fences like an additional member of the hunting pack to corner and bring down larger prey like kudu. This learned behaviour is not unique to wild dogs however and has been observed in lions as well.*

All consuming *(this spread): African wild dogs are voracious feeders, consuming their prey quickly to avoid detection from scavengers and other predators. Everything is eaten and often only small telltale signs remain to give clues to the site of a kill, like an impala's ear or bloodstained grass.*

An unwanted signpost *(above): Vultures like this African white-backed often attract other predators to wild dog kills. Wild dogs deal with this by feeding quickly and moving on but these birds can be a real menace if they become attracted by the scraps of food around a den site. Inquisitive lions need no second invitation to dig-up a wild dog den.*

Evil epitomised? *(opposite): The arrival of the great white hunter in Africa from the late 1800s onwards spelled disaster for the African wild dog. The ingrained notion among farmers, hunters and even game wardens that these colourful canids are nothing more than cold-blooded killers has proved hard to shift.*

Lucky escape *(this spread): This wild dog dispersed from a pack in Botswana and was tracked down to a farm in South Africa. Luckily, the farmer picked up his phone and not his gun, calling in EWT wild dog researcher John Power.*

Where there's a will, there's a way *(above): Wild dogs are known for their ability to dig under fences. This can land them in trouble if they leave the sanctity of a protected reserve yet it also means that they can leave hostile land just as easily.*

Community relations *(right): Following up on a report of wild dogs breaking out onto neighbouring farmland, EWT researcher John Power reads the tracks left in the sand along a farm fenceline.*

Wild dog packs occupy enormous home ranges, far larger than the territories of their larger feline neighbours. This, coupled with their ability to effortlessly slip through or dig under fences, makes the species difficult to contain within the boundaries of protected reserves. Furthermore, with individual dogs or small single-sex groups periodically dispersing from these territories across vast distances to start new packs, wild dogs are primed to come into contact with swelling human settlements as well as hunting and commercial farming land. Here, their reputation as relentless hunters means that they are rarely welcomed. And while this reputation may not be totally unfounded on the basis that wild dogs have been known to occasionally prey on smaller livestock like sheep and goats, research carried out by Dr Greg Rasmussen, director and founder of Zimbabwe's Painted Dog Conservation, does suggest that livestock predation does not occur as often as farmers believe it to. In fact, there have even been documented occasions of packs of wild dogs ignoring the presence of livestock in favour of pursuing more common prey.

With conservation aims for an increase in wild dog numbers across an ever-more commercially driven Africa, this human-predator frontier of conflict is not just going to disappear. The predatory disposition of wild dogs means that they seldom scavenge and so are not easily poisoned or attracted to traps as with other unwelcome visitors to farm and hunting land. Instead, they fall victim to the firearm or explosive devices that are used to destroy dens, sometimes with pups still inside. However, if landowners can be encouraged to pick up the phone instead of a gun then the swift extraction and relocation of wild dogs from unprotected land can be ensured. While this action would help to arrest the decline in wild dog numbers, safe passages through farm or community land would need to be identified and then negotiated for wild dogs dispersing between isolated protected areas in order to actually develop the population. This would promote both the flow of diverse genes between fragmented populations and increased cooperation between neighbouring land users. With open engagement often the preferred choice over mutual attrition between conservation and commercial parties nowadays, perhaps at least tolerance of one another and of this charismatic carnivore has a realistic chance.

Engagement also brings with it the responsibility of education. With wild dogs implicated by landowners for attacks on game and livestock, it is essential for the management of perceptions as well as for the potential payment of any compensation for losses to livestock that the correct species is identified in the case of an attack. In the majority of cases, the more common spotted hyena, black-backed jackal and side-striped jackal are responsible for such attacks instead. Even the domestic dog – a favourite pet, trusted hunting companion and supposed guardian of livestock against attacks from predators – is perhaps more likely to snatch an easy meal from a farmer than a wild dog is, given the rarity of the latter. Attacks by wild dogs on humans are occasionally reported in rural and farming communities too yet, when investigated, it is again proven that other, more common predators are to blame.

One theory as to why the African wild dog is blamed for so many attacks is that the name 'wild dog' can be misunderstood as a term to encompass all wild, dog-like carnivores such as wolves, hyenas, jackals and African wild dogs. It is easy to see how such a name can become lost in translation when one considers that in the wild dog's present range, at least 35 official languages are

A case of mistaken identity *(this spread): Reports of sightings and attacks on livestock by wild dogs from rural communities or farmers can be unreliable as they are often confused with other more common species such as spotted hyena (above) and the smaller black-backed jackal (left) and side-striped jackal.*

spoken, not to mention the hundreds of other local languages. The term 'wild' also tends to evoke thoughts of feral dogs in the minds of many who are unaware of the species' existence. For this reason there are calls from some quarters of the conservation community in those countries that use the name 'wild dog' for the species to be rebranded and for one of the other widely used names, such as 'painted dog' or 'hunting dog', to be adopted.

Even though many perceptions of wildlife and the practices of conservation have developed in the last century or more, these highly sociable canids continue to fare badly. Wild dogs are targeted largely for their perceived incompatibility with human development. Nowadays, the rationale behind the persecution of the species is influenced more by commercial factors rather than what was once the ethical irony of man killing for pleasure and judging a wild animal killing to survive. And if managers of protected game reserves cannot see the value of the wild dog, what chance do the few remaining populations have?

For the wild dog it is fortunate that there are those who still see beyond the financial value of an animal and recognise their duty to protect every cog in the ecosystem and offer a safe haven to a species in trouble. In 2007, after repeatedly breaking out

***Boundless energy and tails held high** (this spread): Despite cutting an intimidating presence when excited, wild dogs are mostly shot because they are seen as a threat to livestock, not man.*

onto neighbouring land, a pack from South Africa's Marakele National Park was safely darted and translocated to Botswana's Northern Tuli Game Reserve. This operation is testament to how solutions can be found for dogs dispersing onto unprotected land given the tolerance, time and resources. And, while for now the future of Africa's wild dog population may rely somewhat ironically on the gun in its dart-projecting form, it is hoped that through landscape-scale conservation efforts there will come a time when wild dogs will be able to move freely between protected populations without fear of the bullet.

Bound by the gun *(this spread): The removal of these dogs from land in South Africa was by the use of a gun. Thankfully, for this pack, it was to tranquillise the dogs and translocate them over the border to Tuli, in Botswana.*

Size
Matters
the dogs of Venetia Limpopo

Reading the signs (previous spread): Sharing their domain with a full complement of large predators means that the wild dogs of Venetia Limpopo Nature Reserve are constantly alert for the signs of danger.

Run to the hills (above): Researchers on South Africa's Venetia Limpopo Nature Reserve noticed that wild dogs were using the reserve's rocky hills both as vantage points for spotting prey on the plains below and as a refuge for avoiding lions.

In their wild environment, wild dogs stand somewhere in the predator hierarchy above jackals but below lions. When there is conflict with leopards or hyenas it often becomes a game of numbers and circumstance. Being more sociable and a pack hunter, wild dogs can usually intimidate a lone hyena on open ground and some packs seem to even take pleasure in chasing leopards up trees. With such a physical size difference though, their relationship with lions is far more one-sided. Even with population densities and the availability of data affecting the consistency of statistics from study sites across the continent, it is believed that lions may be responsible for around a quarter of all wild dog deaths in the wild. Knowing lions actively seek out and dig up wild dog dens, it is perhaps not surprising that this figure is much higher when looking solely at the causes of death in youngsters. And so, as it does wherever lions and wild dogs coexist, the rule that size really does matter governs life on Venetia Limpopo Nature Reserve.

Here, competition for food and space from other top predators echoes the same natural pressures felt by wild dogs living across the continent for millennia and continues to generate day-to-day challenges. However, living on a genetic island cut-off by increasing human development is a very modern dilemma. Over time, inbreeding and the resulting degradation of the gene pool becomes a very real threat. To compound this isolation, as the natural urge to breed drives young wild dogs to disperse and search for others to establish new packs with, so the threats of being hit by vehicles on national roads or being shot for straying onto farming and hunting land come into play. The ten years of wild dog research carried out on Venetia Limpopo shows that, in many ways, the situation on this reserve in South Africa's northern-most Province is a microcosm of the challenges facing the survival of the species across Africa today.

During this period of intense research, Endangered Wildlife Trust (EWT) researchers documented a technique employed by the reserve's wild dogs to keep themselves safe from attack by other predators. When analysing their data, the researchers also started to notice patterns developing in the pack's movements. South Africa's Limpopo Valley is characterised by sandstone

Rocky refuge *(above): The beautifully scenic Limpopo River Valley along South Africa's northern borders with Botswana and Zimbabwe is lined by sandstone ridges and hills, perfect refuge for wild dogs desperate to avoid their feline adversaries.*

hills known locally as 'koppies' and in a habit christened by the researchers as 'koppie hopping' the dogs were recorded making regular, systematic use of these hills to rest and to even den in between hunting on the plains below.

Each day, the small pack would rise early from its resting spot and set out on its quest for food. Being crepuscular, wild dogs prefer to be active in the twilight hours – the perfect time to avoid both their larger nocturnal neighbours and the heat of the African sun. Eventually, even if hunting had been unsuccessful, the pack would make its way to high ground to rest in relative comfort and safety. This habit of systematically taking to the hills is not necessarily typical wild dog behaviour but it was a habit ingrained in the psyche of alpha female Stellar through a mix of desperation and resourcefulness.

Stellar's behaviour was hardly surprising when taking into account her own life story and the changes that occurred in the Venetia Limpopo wild dog population after her arrival at the helm – most of which were by the tooth and claw of her larger feline foes. Stellar was translocated to Venetia Limpopo from Madikwe Game Reserve in South Africa's North West Province after her alpha mate and entire litter of pups were killed there. In the months that followed, researchers at Madikwe watched Stellar roam the reserve's Dwarsberg Mountains alone. Did her desperate existence in Madikwe's hills influence her behaviour as the leader of the pack on Venetia Limpopo?

The Venetia Limpopo pack had become a band of survivors. Along with Stellar, its few remaining members had all seen those closest to them meet a grim end in a struggle with another large carnivore. Avoiding lions had become a priority for all of them and heading to the hills seemed the only option.

Committed to conserve *(right): EWT researcher John Power searches for a signal from a radio collar from the top of Edmondsburg, the highest point on Venetia Limpopo Nature Reserve. Keeping up with a nervous Stellar and her diminished pack meant going where no 4x4 could go.*

Size matters *(following spread): Being much larger and relying on stealth, lions are a constant threat to wild dogs. Around a quarter of all wild dog deaths in the wild can be attributed to lions.*

Rory, the youngest dog in the Venetia Limpopo pack, was Stellar's only surviving offspring from a litter of just four pups in 2007. As a result of having no siblings to play with and living a life on the run, Rory had to grow up fast. Whether all of his siblings died in the jaws of lions is not known for certain but the deaths of other pack members during a period of high lion activity on the reserve certainly unnerved Stellar. When she fell pregnant the following year, her desperation to avoid her den being detected by lions was obvious. Wild dogs usually choose old warthog or aardvark burrows as den sites but, mirroring the pack's daily habit, Stellar chose to head for the sanctity of her territory's inaccessible sandstone hills to make her den.

Wild dogs are known to abandon a den in favour of a new site when the pups are old enough to move short distances with the pack. This relocation distances them from the build-up of scat and any left over food that could attract unwanted attention, first from scavenging birds and then from the lions and hyenas that so often follow. Whatever it was that was unsettling her at her carefully chosen hilltop den site, Stellar was showing signs that she was anxious to move. Perhaps she knew that despite being safer from lions, hills are also a favourite habitat for leopard and hyena. Amazingly, she decided to move her litter some ten kilometres from one den to another – a huge distance for such young legs.

At first, the move seemed to pay off with the adults relaxed and hunting together to provide food for the seven pups. This peaceful existence was short-lived however and the adults were soon forced to defend the pups during a fierce altercation with an opportunistic brown hyena. Disaster may have been prevented and the scavenger seen off but it was an ominous omen for what was to come. Ten long days later and Stellar's mate and five of her pups were dead. In the wake of the hyena clash, the pack was understandably unsettled and ran straight into a pride of lions in the south of the reserve. Although Stellar, Rory and Fender (another adult female) managed to flee with two of the litter,

In his prime *(left): Abel strides purposefully into the warm evening light shortly after his release with another male, Baker, onto Venetia Limpopo Nature Reserve. Unfortunately, despite mating with Stellar, his reign as alpha male was short-lived.*

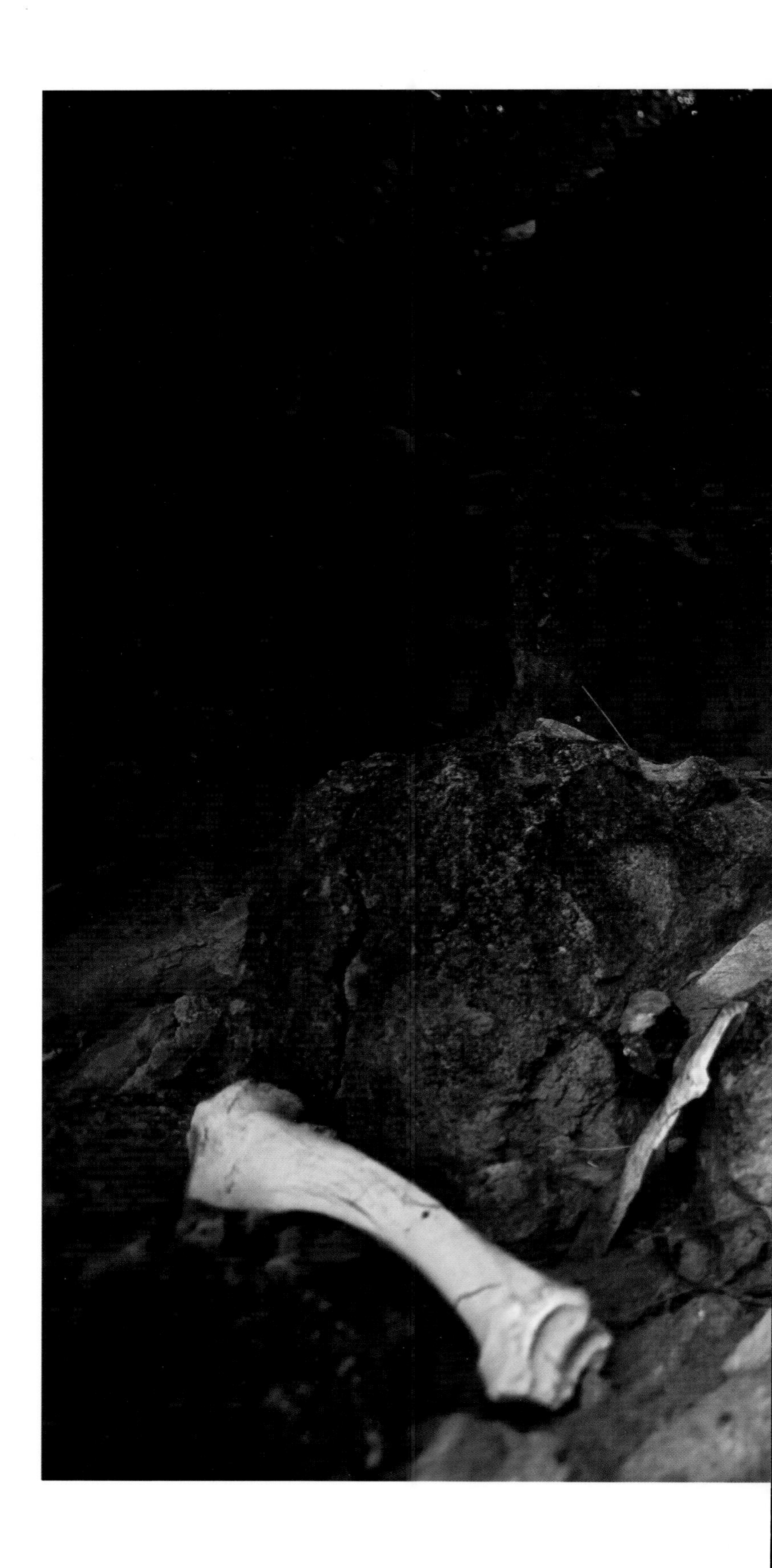

alpha male Budzatjie was killed defending his five offspring. Agonisingly, Stellar lost both of her two remaining pups in the days that followed.

And so began a new, difficult era for the surviving pack of dogs. Not only had such a strong lion presence on the reserve brought direct conflict but the pack was also working harder than ever to find prey, hunt successfully and hold onto their kills when challenged by scavengers. To complicate matters, the only male in the group of survivors was Rory, the son of luckless alpha female Stellar. Would Rory's experiences and maturity lead him to step into the shoes of his father as alpha male and jeopardise maintaining the genetic integrity of this sub-population against the goals of the metapopulation project?

With Rory starting to show signs of ascendancy, the decision was made to introduce two new males to the Venetia Limpopo wild dog pack in the hope that one of them would take on the alpha male mantle, breed with Stellar and form a stronger unit. But would they all bond and would the new boys – the older and larger Abel and Baker – accept Rory and his budding bravado?

***Searching for Abel** (this spread): With the pack split and Stellar below ground ready to give birth, the race was on to understand what had happened to Abel. Researcher John Power searched high, low and even in this cave, the home of a clan of brown hyena and the final resting place of Ringo, another ill-fated alpha male.*

Under the watchful eyes of the researchers, Abel and Baker were successfully bonded in the boma with the two females, Stellar and Fender. At first, Rory was kept in an adjoining boma and his interaction at the fenceline with the two newcomers was watched carefully. When it was clear that he was happy to take his place as a subordinate below Abel, who had emerged as the new dominant male, Rory was then introduced to the pack.

For a while, all seemed rosy on Venetia Limpopo with the pack hunting a variety of prey from scrub hare and the slight steenbok up to large kudu bulls. Stellar, Fender and Rory showed Abel and Baker their technique of chasing prey towards the fences, a strategy used by other predators elsewhere in Africa, as well as their habit of retiring to the hills to rest. But Stellar was starting to keep the pack up on high ground for longer periods than usual and with her exploring caves and crevices it became clear that Abel hadn't wasted any time in mating with her. It was also clear that Stellar was once again intent on gambling against the threat from hyena and leopard to keep her litter as far away from lions as possible.

Sadly, Stellar's luck was not about to change. Her preoccupation with finding a den site as inaccessible to lions as possible had led her pack right into a leopard's domain. Once again, it was her alpha mate who paid the ultimate price. Researchers searched for Abel for days on end. Finally, the knell of the mortality signal given off by his radio collar revealed the hilltop location of his ravaged body.

The necropsy carried out on Abel's body revealed multiple puncture wounds from the canines of his assailant. Bites to his hindquarters hinted to a surprise attack while the deep wounds inflicted on the throat told of the lethal, suffocating bite. Of all Abel's injuries, it was the cleaner penetrations of his skull that

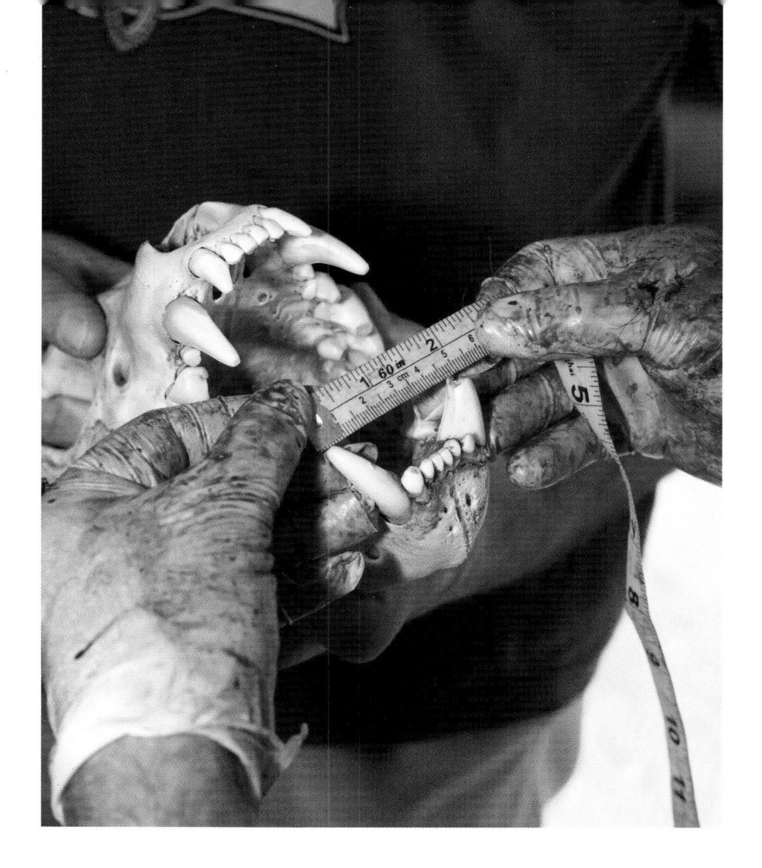

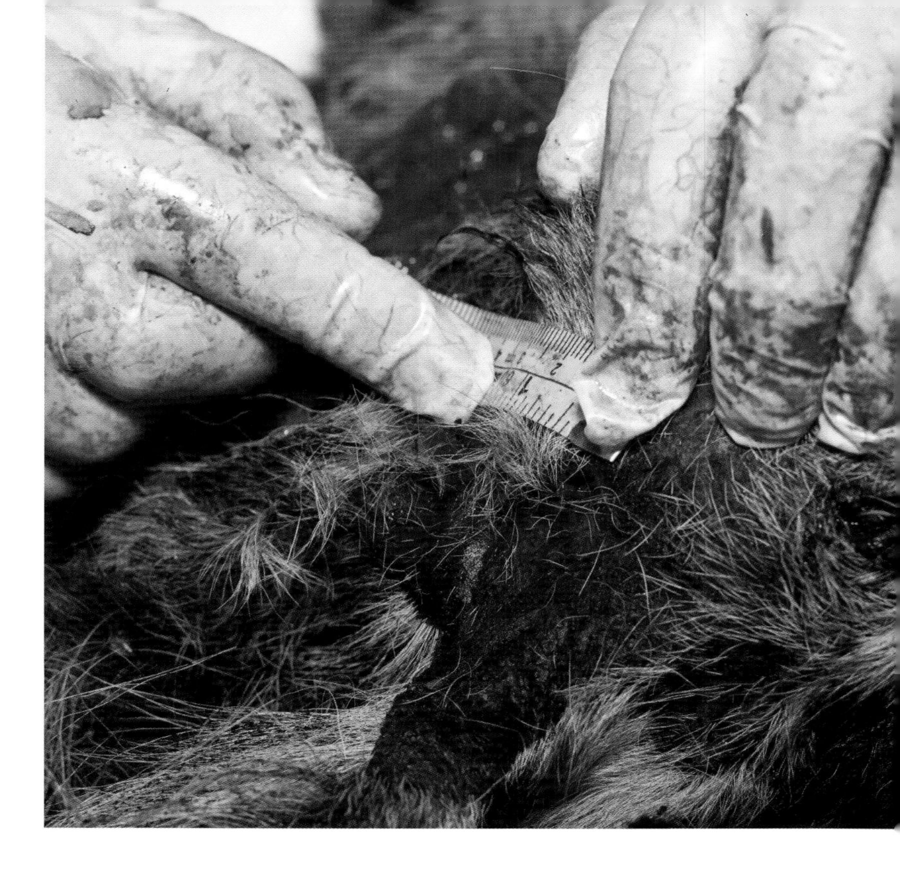

A grim discovery *(clockwise from top left): Researchers perform a necropsy on Abel's body (top left), measure the gauge of the canines on the skull of a brown hyena, a possible suspect (above), and compare it against the distance between puncture wounds to the top of Abel's head, neck and hindquarters (above right), before reflecting the neck skin to reveal the deep puncture wounds (right).*

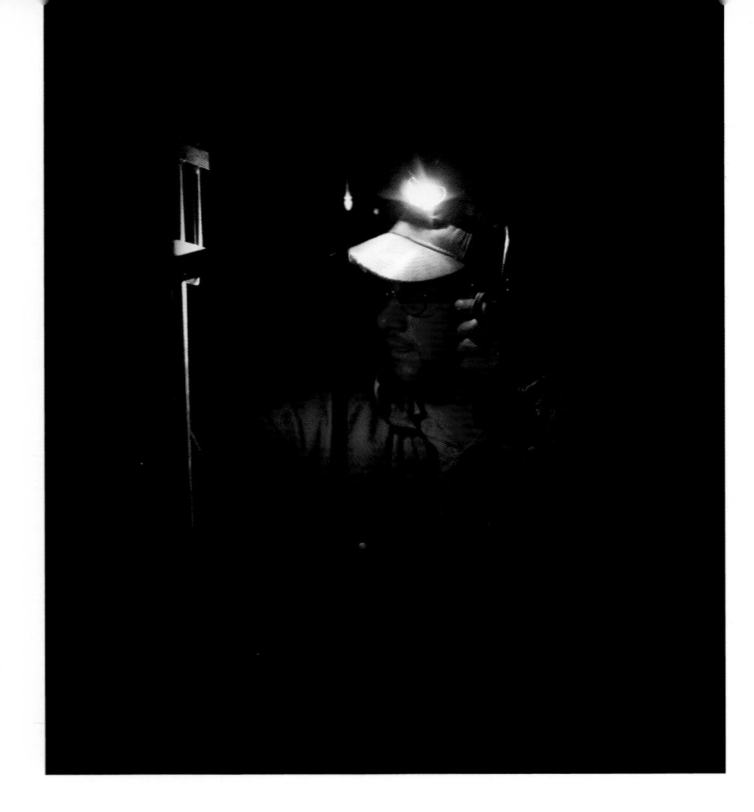

The long hunt begins *(above and top): The attack on Abel split the pack. Was Stellar alone because she was in a den with pups? And could the rest of the pack catch enough prey to survive? Concerned for the pack's safety, the research team searched day and night.*

Silent killer *(right): From the wounds inflicted on Abel's ravaged body, researchers were able to piece together the identity of his assailant – the leopard.*

eventually helped to betray the identity of the killer. Keeping their emotions checked by professionalism and responsibility, the team of researchers were able to measure the gauge of the puncture wounds in Abel's skull and match them against known dental measurements from other large carnivores. This evidence effectively eliminated lions as possible suspects owing to their much larger jaws. That Abel's body was left otherwise intact also cast doubt on whether either brown or spotted hyenas could have been responsible. Brown hyenas had carried off and eaten Abel's alpha forerunner Ringo but this was only after Ringo had been fatally injured hunting warthog. Brown hyenas were also known to shadow the movements of the pack but this behaviour was primarily to steal an easy meal from the more efficient wild dogs. Finally, when taking into account the nature and location of the attack, the size of the wounds and the killing bite to the throat, it was possible to deduce that Abel had probably been killed by a leopard while resting with the pack up in the hills.

There was no doubt that Abel's death would upset the balance of the pack once again, only this time it happened in a way that no one could predict. When the pack was tracked down some days after the attack on Abel, Stellar was missing. Had she also been injured in the melee? Had she already established a den and given birth to pups and if so, why were the others not with her? What was certain was that if Stellar did have a litter hidden away somewhere, she would desperately need the support of the rest of the pack to hunt and bring her food. Even then, without the experience of Abel and with Fender carrying a nasty leg injury from a hunt, Rory and Baker would struggle to catch enough prey just for themselves, especially with prey numbers at their lowest toward the end of the dry season. To make matters worse, Baker's condition also seemed to be deteriorating and he was noticeably slower than Rory and Fender. Was Baker's condition a reaction to the stress of the attack on Abel or was he actually mourning the loss of his companion?

Stellar needed to make contact with the pack soon or she would be putting herself at risk. Also, the longer she spent away from the pack the more chance there would be of Fender usurping her as alpha female. She needed the others and they needed her.

With Stellar not wearing a radio collar, what followed was a long, arduous search for any sign of her and it promised to be a search that would test the knowledge, intuition and tracking skills of the researchers. There were neither fresh tracks nor any signs of a den on the hill where the pack had been spending time before Abel was killed. However, after all of the commotion she could easily have found a different den site. If they were to find Stellar, there was only one option for the research team – to cover as much ground as possible, starting with the landscape around the site of the leopard attack. Efforts intensified with De Beers' game scouts joining in the search to check for any tracks in sandy riverbeds, on game paths and on dirt tracks. After all, wild dogs aren't stupid and will often stick to the more easy-going, open ground when moving through the bush.

Finally, when Stellar's somewhat slighter frame was tracked down a week later it was clear that she hadn't eaten in some time. Her high-pitched, repeated 'hoo-call' that wild dogs use when lost or communicating over long distances signalled her desperation to find the rest of her pack. She had clearly picked up their scent and was moving quickly in their direction at a speed impossible to follow at through the thick mopane bush. Bizarrely, when she did eventually catch up with Rory, Fender and Baker, who by this time were making good use of the full moon to hunt successfully, she didn't stay with them long before heading off on her own again.

Stellar kept up this pattern over the weeks that followed, leaving the pack each day for long periods. Was it a sign that she still had a litter somewhere? Surely, she couldn't keep them alive on her own. After all, in normal wild dog society, raising a litter of pups is a responsibility the whole pack takes very seriously with every adult taking on a role of food provider or babysitter.

The time that Stellar spent on her own gradually lessened. No one will ever know whether she had been trying to prolong Abel's short influence on life at Venetia Limpopo by bringing

***The beginning of the end** (left): Baker's lifeless body lies prostrate on the Venetia Limpopo plains. His unexplained death was just the latest in a long sequence of unfortunate tragedies and spelled the beginning of the end for Stellar's once mighty pack.*

up his pups but all the signs pointed towards this luckless alpha female having lost another litter. And in the context of declining national and international populations, this was not only another big loss for Stellar but a tragedy that reinforces how important each remaining wild dog is.

With the injury to Fender's leg healing and the promise of new life coming to Venetia Limpopo with the spring rains, the timing couldn't have been better for Stellar, Fender, Rory and Baker to reunite. For almost six months they thrived, hunting their favourite prey and surviving as a unit. Unfortunately, Abel's death was not the last tragedy to befall Stellar's dwindling pack though. EWT researcher John Power found Baker's body early one morning in February 2010. Even though the cause of his death will forever remain a mystery after inconclusive necropsy findings, one certainty to arise from Baker's demise was that this latest in a series of unfortunate events spelled the end of the line for Stellar's pack on Venetia Limpopo Nature Reserve. Once again, Rory had found himself as the only male in his mother's pack and if the genetic integrity of South Africa's remaining wild dog packs was to be maintained, he had to be separated from Stellar. He had survived when all of his siblings had met savage ends and had led the pack in hunts in Stellar's absence. All the signs were there that Rory would one day ascend to lead a pack. In a wilderness unconstrained by human infrastructure it is likely that he would have already dispersed on his own accord to find a new pack and to breed. However, with him living in a corner of South Africa feeling increasing pressure from human industry and infrastructure, Rory's fate would be discussed and decided upon around a table in a meeting room. Fortunately, that meeting would be between members of the Wild Dog Advisory Group and between people with his best interests and the future of his species at heart.

Sole survivor *(above): Rory had seen much of his family perish in the jaws of predators and had developed into an adept hunter. If his experiences were to be the foundations for him becoming an alpha male one day, it would have to be as the leader of a different pack.*

Luckless leader *(opposite): Despite her best efforts, Stellar had lost three alpha mates and all but one pup from four litters. She epitomised what it meant to be an underdog.*

Intervening in the life of a wild dog pack is never ideal and is clearly not a decision or responsibility any conservationist takes lightly. But, with more and more protected areas dropping their fences with neighbouring reserves to form greater conservation areas, hopefully there will be less of a necessity for the physical translocation of wild dogs in the future and natural movement between packs can take place. It was hoped that fences between Venetia Limpopo and South Africa's Mapungubwe National Park would be dropped during Stellar's time on the reserve. This would have linked the pack through Mapungubwe to the wild dogs living in Botswana's Tuli area. However, it would have been unfair to make Stellar and Fender wait for state veterinary red tape to be cleared and for the fences to come down. It was not likely that a pack of just two females would have lasted long on their own, particularly knowing the pack's track record. Fittingly, like Rory before them, they were given the chance of a fresh start in KwaZulu-Natal and the opportunity to build a new pack.

Transcending Boundaries

wild dogs in a modern landscape

The days are becoming numbered for the practice of fencing off a tract of land, permanently separating all of its wild inhabitants from the outside world and labelling it as a conservation area. Of course this does remain a necessary approach in areas where protected land is hemmed-in by hostile neighbours, dangerous human infrastructure or expanding communities. However, as this practice becomes more exclusively aligned with private game farms and commercial hunting land, conservationists and landowners around the world are recognising the benefits of opening their doors to wildlife tourism and removing their fences with neighbouring protected land.

This collaborative, landscape-scale approach to conservation is not a new concept for Africa or for the Southern African region however. Following IUCN's identification of protected areas sharing common borders in the late 1980s, authorities in South Africa and Botswana worked to bring the management of what is now the Kgalagadi Transfrontier Park under one management plan. The park was officially launched in 2000, two years before the Heads of State of South Africa, Mozambique and Zimbabwe unveiled the Great Limpopo Transfrontier Park, incorporating Mozambique's Limpopo, Zimbabwe's Gonarezhou and South Africa's Kruger National Parks.

In late 2008 the United Nations Environment Programme (UNEP) upgraded the African wild dog's status to migratory, along with that of its feline neighbour the cheetah. It was agreed at the 9th Convention on Migratory Species that the wild dog has such an unfavourable conservation status that cooperation is required between nations for the conservation of the species. The decisions made at the convention not only promise to afford the wild dog greater protection but also call for further regional cooperation and the formulation of international agreements. This is particularly pertinent to Southern Africa where many of the remaining wild dog populations live near international boundaries. As a result, the vast territories held by packs and the natural inclination of small groups to disperse great distances to form new packs are known to take wild dogs across borders. When this happens, it is essential for the future of the species to know that they are crossing into friendly territory.

In turn, it is hoped that these landmark decisions will go on to influence the formation of new transfrontier conservation areas across Africa. By providing species that need a lot of space, like the wild dog, with the land necessary to follow their natural dispersal and migratory patterns, so the opportunity is created to develop genetically viable populations. One area that is the focus of such coordinated efforts is the Greater Mapungubwe Transfrontier Conservation Area (TFCA), an area that is made up of land from South Africa, Botswana and Zimbabwe with

The Limpopo-Shashe confluence *(previous spread): The meeting of these two great river systems also signifies the meeting point of South Africa, Zimbabwe and Botswana and the centre of a transfrontier conservation area (TFCA) in the making.*

Natural boundary *(opposite): The valley of the Limpopo River is rich in wildlife and greater protection could see the formation of a viable wild dog population, especially as lion numbers are low here.*

A bright future? *(above): Following a landmark decision by UNEP to afford the wild dog greater protection as a migratory species that crosses international boundaries, will these pups born in the sanctity of the Limpopo riverine forest in Botswana grow up and disperse safely to make their home in neighbouring South Africa or Zimbabwe?*

the meeting of the Limpopo and Shashe rivers at its core. The establishment of this area would officially link two populations of wild dogs already safely within the metapopulation and could provide a safe future for the small number of dogs known to be living a dangerous life outside of protected reserves in the Limpopo region.

The area already has a reputation for providing a home and a future for wild dogs after the successful translocation of a pack from South Africa's Marakele National Park to Botswana's Northern Tuli Game Reserve in 2007. This pack is known to now readily explore the expanse of the burgeoning conservation area in the absence of other packs and has visited the boundary of the Venetia Limpopo Nature Reserve boundary on a number of occasions. Even with a relatively low lion population in the area however, this exploratory behaviour does not come without its risks.

The threats associated with roads bordering and cutting through protected areas are of great concern to conservationists and a focus of current research. Wild dog specialist Wendy Collinson has turned her focus to researching the threat that road traffic poses to wildlife in the Greater Mapungubwe TFCA. Wild dogs from both Botswana's Northern Tuli Game Reserve and South Africa's Venetia Limpopo Nature Reserve have been killed on a road cutting through the conservation area linking two of South Africa's border posts with Zimbabwe and Botswana. One of the driving forces behind Wendy's research is the threat of increased traffic on this road after South Africa's government approved plans for the development of a coalmine just six kilometres from the boundary of Mapungubwe National Park, the heart of the international conservation area. Wendy hopes that the findings of her research will also help to influence planning decisions in sensitive conservation areas elsewhere in this developing continent. The Serengeti-Mara Ecosystem of East Africa and the Great Limpopo Transfrontier Park of Southern Africa are two

***Hallowed ground** (left): SANParks Cultural Heritage Guide Cedric Setlako looks out across the plains below Mapungubwe Hill, a UNESCO World Heritage Site. The site may be the cultural heart of the Greater Mapungubwe TFCA but developments of a coalmine nearby mean that this is a landscape under threat.*

such areas that continue to feel the pressure of calls for main national roads to be carved through their land. Like the Greater Mapungubwe TFCA, these renowned ecosystems are home to populations of globally threatened species like the African wild dog, African lion and black rhinoceros and roads not only bring the threat of collisions with traffic but also open up protected areas to the threat of poaching.

It is from rural communities neighbouring protected reserves and living along potential dispersal routes that many current threats to wild dog survival are known to come. By and large, such communities are used to living off the land. Mostly, this way of life has been customary yet, in a developing continent with a widening gap between Africa's rich and poor, economic hardship is making taking from the land more of a necessity.

Snares are used in great numbers by hunter-gatherers from these communities poaching for bushmeat. Yet, while the intent may be to catch an antelope or warthog that could feed a family for days or fetch a handsome price at the market, the method of setting dozens of wire snares throughout the bush also leads to the maiming or slow and painful death of countless other species that the poacher often has no interest in eating. Unfortunately, it is the terrestrial predators hunting these same antelope and warthog that all too often get caught up in these circles of death. As a result, this subsistence approach to poaching can have a devastating affect on the overall biodiversity of an area through this kind of secondary impact.

Along with the vast wilderness of Botswana's Okavango Delta, the Great Limpopo Transfrontier Park is one of just two areas in Southern Africa currently large enough to house genetically viable populations of some of Africa's most endangered large mammals. Plans for the park include expansion northwards into Zimbabwe however and it is no secret that the country's wildlife has suffered in the wake of the enduring economic crises there.

***On the road to extinction** (right): EWT researcher Wendy Collinson collects information on a road death in the Limpopo Valley. This road has claimed the lives of a number of wild dogs moving between South Africa and Botswana. With plans for a coal mine in the area, more traffic will mean more tragedies.*

Dog Conservation
LAND ROVER

Ultimately, the Limpopo and Kruger National Parks will link with Gonarezhou, Zimbabwe's second largest National Park, via the Sengwe Corridor. Unfortunately, Gonarezhou National Park is one of the country's conservation areas that continue to feel the destructive affects of poaching. It is believed that it is the park's sheer size that has saved the majority of its wildlife from destruction however, as poaching tends to be concentrated around the outer reaches of such vast parks. The small amount of data that exists on Gonarezhou's wild dog population supports this and suggests that a healthy number of individuals exist in several packs in spite of the threats from poaching. As well as the park's size, another factor likely to contribute to the success of the wild dog population here is the low number of lions.

Early genetic studies of those wild dogs living in Gonarezhou and the rest of Zimbabwe's eastern lowlands seem to show that the population is not genetically connected to those further south in South Africa's Kruger National Park. It is encouraging that despite the long-term pressures placed on Zimbabwe's wildlife, one of the country's great wildernesses could be a major piece in the jigsaw that cements a truly viable future for the African wild dog.

With conservation areas like the Great Limpopo Transfrontier Park spreading across borders into new territories, poaching is not the only threat to wildlife that conservation authorities will have to consider. Domestic dogs are commonly kept as pets,

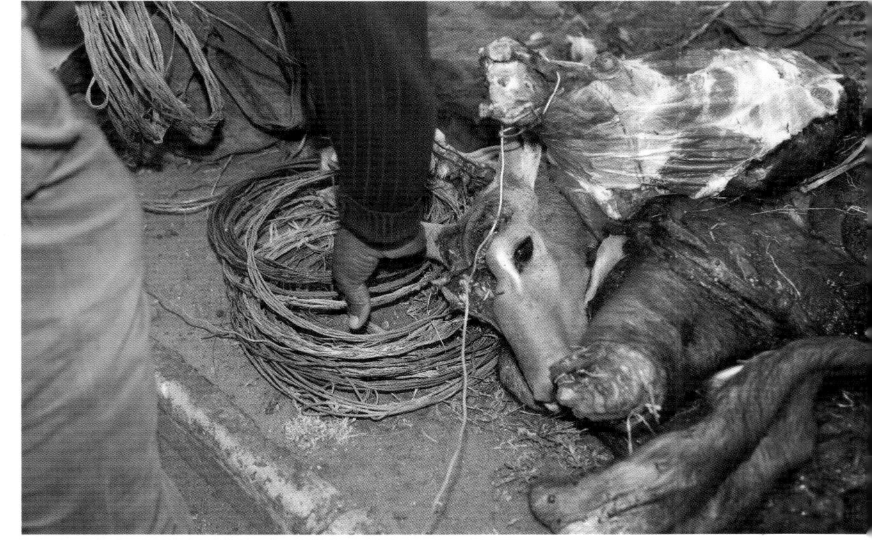

Community relations *(opposite): EWT community liaison officer Sithembiso Ndlovu discusses wild dog activity with the wife of an induna, a community leader in Zululand. With hopes for safe wild dog dispersal routes between reserves and the expansion of conservation areas, a mutual support and understanding between conservation bodies and local communities is essential.*

A poacher's haul *(above and right): The rhino horn and ivory trades hit the international headlines for good reason but neither create superfluous victims in the same way as bushmeat snaring — a very real threat to wild dogs.*

protectors of livestock and hunting hounds by rural communities throughout Africa. Hunters make regular forays with their dogs into protected areas in search of bushmeat. Similarly, when their own land becomes overgrazed, herders will take full advantage of an absence of fences to graze their stock on conservation land, often with their canine companions in tow. Due to the general lack of availability of common veterinary care throughout much of rural Africa however, these domestic dogs often carry and transmit diseases that can be a threat to wildlife.

In parts of Southern and East Africa, populations of wild dogs and other canids, such as bat-eared foxes and black-backed jackals, have been decimated by the transmission of rabies and canine distemper. Wild dogs in particular are known to be more susceptible to these diseases than domestic dogs are. Pre-hunt rallies among excited wild dog pack members involve a lot of biting and goading of muzzles and mouths, perfect behaviour for promoting the rapid spread of rabies and canine distemper that can be transmitted through contact with saliva and airborne respiratory secretions. Other social habits, such as cooperative feeding, can also exacerbate any transmission among a pack. Yet, it was when a strain of the canine distemper virus wiped out many of the Serengeti National Park's lions in Tanzania in 1994 that the extensiveness of the threat from diseases transmitted by domestic dogs living along the boundaries of conservation areas was truly realised.

The game fences that have for so long fortified South Africa's game reserves and national parks and restricted natural animal dispersal and migratory patterns have, on the other hand, served to limit contact between wildlife and the domestic animals of nearby rural communities. In the great, unfenced wildernesses of East Africa however, a more hands-on solution to limiting the spread of disease to sensitive wildlife populations has been necessary. Organisations like the Tusk Trust have focused their efforts on vaccinating the thousands of domestic dogs living in rural villages around Kenya and Tanzania's world-famous conservation areas. Such vaccination programmes bypass many of the financial costs involved in tracking and vaccinating rare and wide-roaming animals like wild dogs, a process that can also cause stress to such susceptible and marginalised species. By vaccinating domestic dogs, the risk of people becoming exposed to diseases such as rabies is also minimised. Tangible human benefits such as this can in turn be used as a means to educate local communities about the value of endangered carnivores like the wild dog. After all, the ability to engage with those people living alongside dangerous and threatened wildlife is one of the most important challenges conservationists face.

***Big mover** (below): An attentive African wild dog trots through the bush close to South Africa's border with Zimbabwe. But will the UN's reclassification of the species as migratory really lead to greater protection when wild dogs do cross human designated boundaries?*

Even though accurately recorded accounts of wild dogs attacking humans are very rare, it is the perceived threat of attack which often forms the basis for persecution from those living alongside Africa's carnivores. With fears for personal safety and the risk of the loss of livestock potentially growing as a result of wild dogs being awarded migratory status and encouraged to cross human borders, conservationists and authorities should be prepared to constructively engage with rural subsistence communities and the commercial farming and hunting sectors.

In South Africa in particular, constructive engagement can be made tricky by the fact that many commercial landowners see the wild dog as worthless since it carries no commercial value. What is more, the financial compensation that can be claimed by farmers in the event of the loss of livestock to lions is not extended in the case of predation by wild dogs. Such factors make the work of a conservationist in a developing and ever more business-savvy Africa more complex. These challenges also reinforce the case that government-level agreements over controversial matters often can't be delivered without the help of people with knowledge of local concerns and who speak local languages.

Building a jigsaw *(above): Brendan Whittington-Jones, coordinator of the KwaZulu-Natal Wild Dog Management Group, is developing a network of safe dispersal routes and wild dog 'friendly zones' between protected areas. Although, keeping track of the region's wide-roaming packs has proven to be a challenge in itself.*

The Endangered Wildlife Trust (EWT) has shown just how effective embracing this local knowledge can be and has been using it to good affect in wild dog conservation. In KwaZulu-Natal, South Africa's eastern-most province, EWT has been working to achieve cooperation with rural communities over transient animals passing between protected populations. For all of South Africa's political, historical and cultural nuances, this task would be close to unachievable for Brendan Whittington-Jones, researcher and coordinator of the KwaZulu-Natal Wild Dog Management Group. For this reason, Brendan has been working alongside EWT community liaison officer Sithembiso Ndlovu who is not only a keen conservation student but is a member of the *amaZulu*, the most numerous and perhaps the most proud ethnic group in South Africa. The work that Brendan and Sithembiso have done educating children in rural KwaZulu-Natal has developed a grass roots understanding of the wild dog and its plight. At the other end of the spectrum, their input at community meetings has helped to develop a trust of their work and has forged agreements, allowing Brendan and Sithembiso to identify on a map wild dog 'friendly zones' between game reserves. Like putting together a jigsaw, Brendan plans to create enough of these zones through this community liaison work that wild dogs will be able to disperse from protected reserves and pass through community land free from the threat of persecution on their way to finding other dogs and forming new packs. If successful, KwaZulu-Natal's wild dog population will become South Africa's second standalone genetically viable breeding population after the Kruger National Park.

The importance of creating a second viable population in South Africa to reversing the decline in wild dog numbers cannot be underestimated. South Africa is widely regarded as Africa's most developed country and is dealing with the challenges of making space for its wildlife in a modern world before many of its African neighbours. The lessons learned in South Africa now

AmaNkentshane *(above): The complexity of the Zulu name for the wild dog is matched in the complexity of the species' status in the KwaZulu-Natal region of South Africa. Loved and loathed, maligned and misunderstood, the wild dog has often struggled to establish a home even in reserves renowned for their conservation outlook.*

are likely to form the basis for wild dog management plans elsewhere on the African continent in years to come. However, community engagement is just one part of a formula necessary for halting the decline in wild dog numbers. Collaboration and the sharing of knowledge between researchers in other parts of the wild dog's range, rather than each working in isolation, can only help to promote a greater understanding of the possibilities and obstacles to developing both local and wider populations.

In early 2011, collaboration between researchers based more than 450 kilometres apart in neighbouring countries brought to light the distances that wild dogs are dispersing to find mates and form new packs. When two new male wild dogs arrived in the Tuli Block in Botswana, Craig Jackson of the Northern Tuli Predator Project circulated pictures in the hope that fellow researchers in the region would be able to identify the dogs from coat patterns. Perhaps expecting a response from northern South Africa or further to the west in Botswana, Craig was amazed to hear from Dr Rosemary Groom in the Save Valley Conservancy in eastern Zimbabwe. The two males had run one of the biggest dispersals ever recorded and this information, made possible through networking and sharing information, has helped to paint a clearer picture of the genetic make up of the Tuli wild dog population and how wild dogs are traversing natural and man-made boundaries to ensure the survival of their species.

Significant research is being carried out in northern Botswana that could make life safer for dispersing wild dogs and for those dogs living in areas beyond the fenced boundaries of protected reserves. The results of the Botswana Predator Conservation Trust's (BPCT) BioBoundary Project could help to alleviate the threats of disease, persecution and road deaths to wild dogs by keeping them off farm and community land. This research, that is being carried out by Dr Peter Apps and Dr Lesego Mmualefe

***Chemical analysis** (above): A wild dog sniffs scent left by another dog. A project in Botswana is working to identify the very chemical components in wild dog urine and faeces that act as territorial signs to other dogs. The project aims to reproduce those chemicals to create synthetic scent boundaries and keep wild dogs from venturing onto land where they could be at risk.*

under the guidance of BPCT founder Dr J.W. 'Tico' McNutt, aims to identify the precise chemical components present in wild dog urine and faeces that act as territorial markers to other dogs. The goal of the Bioboundary Project field work being done in study areas in eastern and northern Botswana, as well as the chemical analysis work in a laboratory in the town of Maun, is to be able to reproduce those chemicals and create artificial, flexible scent boundaries. Acting like road signs to dispersing wild dogs by guiding a safe passage between populations, this synthetic scent marking process represents a manageable and flexible solution to many of the issues influencing African wild dog conservation at a time when the species needs a solution, and fast.

The BioBoundary Project's objectives complement community engagement efforts perfectly in that flexible, synthetic territory boundaries can keep wild dogs away from land where livestock is kept. Yet, that is only part of the solution to managing wild dogs beyond the boundaries of protected reserves. As the land available to wild dogs is increased and dispersal corridors that link conservation areas are opened up, so the populations of prey species like kudu and impala on protected land must be monitored. Predator researchers are increasingly interested in what is known as the 'carrying capacity' of the land where their study animals live. Both the quality and the type of vegetation available to herbivorous prey species determine in turn how many predators can be sustained there. The problem for those people concerned with wild dog conservation is that herbivores like elephant, rhino and buffalo that consume vast amounts of vegetation and are not on the wild dog's menu generate income through tourism. Conservationists will have to become salesmen of the wild dog brand if they are to convince reserve managers of the value of wild dogs and to provide for them. Otherwise, the communities living along dispersal routes that are so crucial to the linking of wild dog populations may find their livestock on the wild dog's menu.

Balancing biomass *(right and overleaf): As safe dispersal routes for wild dogs are opened up to link populations, it will be important to monitor and provide habitat for prey species like impala and kudu to ensure wild dogs don't target livestock. This may mean convincing some landowners to provide for smaller game species over the larger elephants, rhino and buffalo that generate income from tourism.*

Shaping
a Future
are the dog days over?

So, what does the future hold for the African wild dog? Will the development of greater cross-border conservation areas and the reclassification of the species as migratory actually lead to better protection? Or, have we reached a tipping point? Has too much damage been done by wanton persecution that those wild dogs lucky enough to survive are now doing so in such fragmented populations that it's too late to save the species? Moreover, is it even financially viable to try to halt the decline of a top predator with limited appeal to paying tourists? The answer is that we have to at least try to arrest the decline and give wild dogs the space they need to survive on the basis that, morally, it is the right thing to do.

The lessons learned from the reintroduction of the grey wolf into Yellowstone National Park in the United States of America also remind us that the wolf's distant African relative has its place in nature and an effect on the wider ecosystem, no matter how much we may still have to learn about it. Since its return to Yellowstone, the grey wolf has altered the habitat in the park by reducing elk numbers. In turn, this has allowed the park's trees to flourish and re-establish dense stands. The return of willow trees has seen the beaver population boom, leading to improved water quality, and so the chain reaction goes on. Of course, there will be detractors that claim that Africa is home to many other carnivores and that the demise of one top predator would not have as vast an affect as has been felt across the Atlantic in Yellowstone. On the face of things, that may appear to be true yet a look at population trends tells a worrying story. Every other large carnivore on the African continent is in decline too, even lion and leopard that are seen as more charismatic and valued as tourist magnets. No longer can it be assumed that Africa's vast wildernesses and great diversity of species automatically ensure a future for the continent's wildlife.

In many parts of Africa, the area of protected land secured for conservation is growing. This alone should be celebrated but what is most significant for wild dog conservation is the removal of fences between these reserves and the creation of large-scale conservation areas under the guidance and protection of UN legislation. It is an example of the United Nations Environment

Destination unknown? *(opposite): Investigations into trade in wild dogs have brought to light an illegal and lucrative practice of removing pups like this one from dens in the wild to supply the zoo industry. If calls are answered for wild dog trade to be controlled under CITES then in the future we will hopefully only see wild dogs moved from their territories in the wild in crates like this for translocation to other reserves to form new breeding packs.*

Misunderstood? *(previous spread and above): A downward trend in population figures is not unique to wild dogs. Every large African carnivore is in decline while the reintroduction of grey wolves to Yellowstone National Park in the USA has triggered a chain reaction of ecological events showing the benefit of top predators to the wider ecosystem. Does Africa need to rethink how it values predators?*

Programme's (UNEP) efforts being translated into action on the ground. However, an increasing number of people believe that UNEP's responsibilities towards conserving the wild dog do not stop at simply calling for greater collaboration between conservation authorities in neighbouring countries and for an increase in land provision. UNEP administers the secretariat of CITES, the Convention on International Trade in Endangered Species of Wild Fauna and Flora. Calls for the wild dog to be listed and protected under CITES have been increasingly louder and from a growing base of concerned international public since an undercover investigation into wild dog trade was published in early 2010.

The existing legal trade in wild dogs that serves zoos worldwide does offer a future for many animals bred and reared in captivity at breeding centres. This is because, unfortunately, many wild dogs bred at such places are done so with little or no thought to genetic management, resulting in wild dog stock that is unfit for release back into a wild environment. Yet, the investigation published in 2010 was sparked following the removal of wild dog litters from dens in the wild in Zimbabwe at the request and expense of South African traders. The conditions in which these vulnerable pups were smuggled out of the country meant that, of the litters recovered by wildlife crime officers, only a small number of pups actually survived. While there continues to be reservations over certain accuracies in the investigation report, it undoubtedly highlights the effect that current wild dog trade is having on the wild population as some traders look to enrich their captive stock with new bloodlines. With Africa's wild dog population tumbling towards just 3,000 individuals, CITES must now play its part in safeguarding the future of the species by adding it to the list of roughly 5,000 animal species that are protected against exploitation by international trade.

As the smuggling of live pups across international borders and the destruction of dens by farmers show, protective legislation is not enough without a greater understanding and sense of value,

***Inspiring the next generation** (right): Many organisations are complementing their conservation efforts with local education work. The focus and timing of EWT's education work in KwaZulu-Natal is well placed in a region with a growing wild dog population.*

particularly among those living alongside such a controversial species. Educating and inspiring children is an essential element of forging a future for wild dogs in the new South Africa. Wild dogs will always need conservation champions in a developing landscape and this is something that both the Botswana Predator Conservation Trust (BPCT) and the Endangered Wildlife Trust (EWT) have clearly recognised. Ingrained perceptions are not changed overnight and are often harder to break down in older members of communities and so to achieve a widespread, long-term change of mindset towards wild dogs, it is young people that must be inspired.

The wild dog population is steadily increasing in the Hluhluwe Imfolozi Park, the flagship reserve of South Africa's KwaZulu-Natal Province. As a result, there is a growing need to create safe dispersal passages through community land that will link the park to the network of other protected sites elsewhere in the province. This joined-up network of wild dog friendly areas will minimise the need for human intervention in the maintenance of a genetically healthy population. However, the plans of the KwaZulu-Natal Wild Dog Management Group can only be fully realised through careful community engagement and education work. A key factor in the success of these plans in a part of South Africa staunchly proud of its Zulu heritage is the recognition and utilisation of the skills of a member of the *amaZulu* as a community liaison officer. In time, this could well prove to be a model for engaging constructively with those communities that live in or alongside sensitive conservation areas elsewhere in Africa. After all, a noticeable shift has been made within the conservation movement away from outdated and authoritarian conservation practices towards a more holistic approach. The modern conservationist needs to be mindful of cultural nuances as well as listening to and accepting the concerns of landowners in an increasingly economy-driven landscape.

Living without boundaries *(this spread): If the wide-roaming wild dog is to have a future in a rapidly developing continent, that vision is likely to include land beyond the borders of protected reserves and see packs making less use of fence-lines and more use of natural boundaries like river courses.*

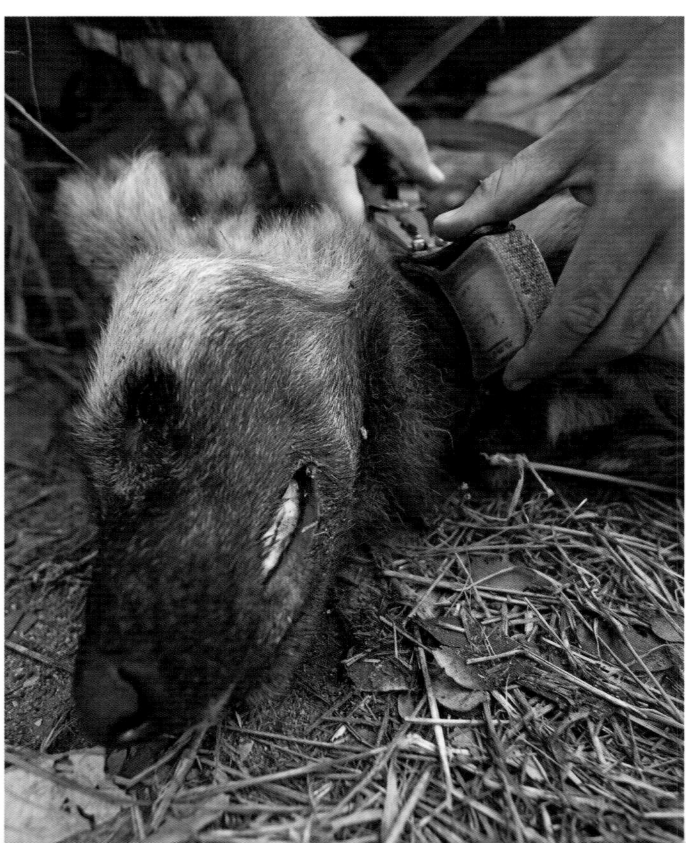

Community engagement and an awareness of local values and cultures are not the only areas in which conservationists and researchers are having to develop their skills. Researchers are being used more and more by the media as presenters or journalists to tell stories from the front line. The ability to deal with and influence the media has therefore become an equally important skill for a conservationist in this day and age. This rings particularly true for those working to protect a terrestrial predator with a questionable reputation. The African wild dog is in desperate need of a rebranding. In harnessing the powers of traditional print and broadcast media alongside the social and digital platforms of new media, conservationists have perhaps never had a greater opportunity to turn around the fortunes of this remarkable species. The change in fortune and reputation of other species shows that it can be done, too. Naturally, these things take some time but the resurgence of the red kite in the United Kingdom, for example, is largely down to a coordinated reintroduction programme working alongside a PR campaign to change public perspective. Once persecuted to near extinction, this bird of prey is now seen by many as a magnificent, graceful icon of the skies in a country with a long and strange relationship with any species of a predatory disposition.

Closer to home for the wild dog, the Ethiopian wolf may still be classified as endangered but an international awareness of its plight has occurred relatively recently, coinciding largely with its name being changed from that of 'Simien jackal'. Yet, for the Ethiopian wolf, this has been no mere name changing exercise, this has been a rebranding. Having been identified by scientists through DNA testing as closely related to the coyote and grey wolf, the Ethiopian wolf has joined its close relatives and has become an iconic symbol of the wilderness. For many people around the world, the wolf captures the imagination in a way that a jackal or fox never will. While this may be unfair on the jackal, could a similar change help to reverse the fortunes of *Lycaon pictus*? There are many in the world of conservation who think that it could. The most mooted change is altering the common English name to that of 'painted dog' so that it is at least consistent with its Latin species name. Advocates for this change also argue that moving away from the name 'wild dog'

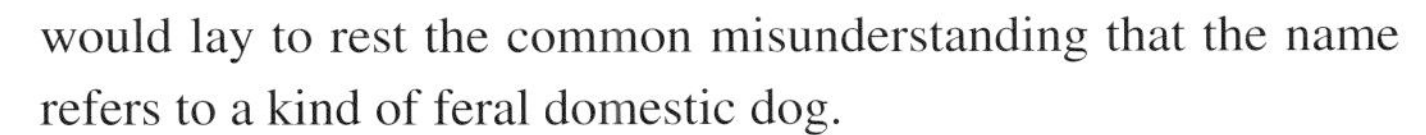

would lay to rest the common misunderstanding that the name refers to a kind of feral domestic dog.

Many believe that the change should not stop there. Indeed, the name 'painted wolf' is not only a more accurate translation of its scientific name but, as with the Ethiopian wolf, the name aligns the species with some of its closest relatives. With international media still using a confusing array of names, including 'wild dogs', 'hunting dogs' and 'painted dogs', perhaps the time is now right for those researching and working to conserve the African wild dog to collaborate not only through the sharing of knowledge and data but on the consolidation of the identity of *Lycaon pictus*. Surely, such a charismatic, active and intensely sociable animal can be represented more consistently in the world's media? This should not be overlooked as a goal for conservation bodies and landowners alike with the potential for more responsible media coverage positively influencing public interest and investment opportunities.

***Embracing change** (opposite page): Researchers are making use of practical technology like GPS collars and devices to improve our understanding of species behaviour. This technology is particularly useful to those working to understand the movements of species like the wild dog that cover such vast distances.*

***The power of mobile technology** (above, left): EWT community liaison officer Sithembiso Ndlovu shows pictures of wild dogs on his cellular phone to a construction worker who had heard news reports of wild dogs attacking children in the area. The reported incident actually involved jackals and the information shared during this chance encounter in rural KwaZulu-Natal helped to influence radio news bulletins later that day and put community fears to rest.*

***Capturing a bigger picture** (above): Camera traps are incredibly useful tools for researchers of animals that are easily recognisable by coat patterns, as wild dogs are. The technology has also allowed wild dog conservationists to build up a greater understanding of those populations living largely undetected outside of protected reserves.*

Identity crisis (opposite): The African wild dog is known by numerous names in English yet here is a growing feeling that an official change to 'painted dog' or 'painted wolf' would help its conservation cause, as well as being more consistent with its scientific name.

The light at the end of the tunnel? *(above): The concept of wild dog tourism is still in relative infancy but if it can be proven that ventures like this one at Venetia Limpopo Nature Reserve can generate income for landowners then more reserves may be willing to reintroduce wild dogs or welcome the natural arrival of dispersed groups.*

Greater investment represents a chance to attain two of those things that conservation bodies often find hard to access – greater human and technological resources. Cameras, tracking equipment, GPS and communication devices are all part of the modern conservationist's arsenal of technology. An ability to use them effectively opens up research opportunities, makes real changes to efficiency and provides a platform for taking life at the front line of conservation to investors and a concerned public. The power of mobile technology platforms like digital cameras, smart phones and laptop devices in the hands of the modern conservationist was made clear one morning in rural

KwaZulu-Natal. While following up on the GPS coordinates of a pack of wild dogs that had dispersed from Hluhluwe Imfolozi Park, Brendan Whittington-Jones and Sithembiso Ndlovu were stopped by a road worker who associated the wording on the side of their EWT research vehicle with a news story that he had heard on a local Zulu radio station earlier that day. The story that was being broadcast focused on two rabid 'wild dogs' that had attacked children in the area and infected them with rabies. Sithembiso was able to show the road worker pictures of African wild dogs on his cellular phone and ask whether the pictures matched the description of the animals given during the radio broadcast. The discussions during this chance encounter and a visit to the radio station to read initial reports revealed that the likely suspects for the attack on the children were jackals. While Sithembiso was able to help the news editors accurately amend their story, the experience exposed some of the problems with the name 'wild dog', particularly in translation.

Technology also opens up new possibilities in eco-tourism. Wildlife guides have used radio telemetry systems for many years to track animals and make sought-after species habituated to tourist vehicles. Until now, this tracking has mainly happened after hours and out of the sight of tourists. Yet, the chance to join researchers at the front line of conservation and track Africa's endangered wildlife is proving an attractive alternative to the regular safari. As a result, tourism now represents one of the greatest factors in securing a future for wild dogs.

In an increasingly money-driven world, it is a sad reality that many people don't value something unless there is a monetary worth assigned to it. With wild dogs having no commercial value attached to them in the way that a kudu has, for example, there is no incentive for commercial landowners to either value them or welcome them on their land. If tourism can formulate some kind of economic value for wild dogs and landowners can see a benefit both commercially and financially, then there is the hope that more suitable conservation areas will open their doors to wild dogs. In turn, like adding more pieces to a jigsaw, this would alleviate the pressure on the existing metapopulation sites and allow for dogs to disperse more freely between protected

reserves with less of a risk from vehicles, snares, persecution, disease and the possibility of inbreeding.

The 'Big Five' of lion, leopard, elephant, rhino and buffalo has become a global marketing brand and these iconic species will always hold a certain fascination for tourists. Many managers of smaller game reserves manage their land almost exclusively to maintain healthy numbers of these species and ensure an equally healthy cash flow through tourism revenue. However, not only are there increasing concerns over this micro-managed method of conservation but less iconic species have become increasingly popular with tourists. A wild dog-based tourism venture at South Africa's Venetia Limpopo Nature Reserve has showed signs that wild dogs can pay their way in the modern world. It is hoped that this venture will be seen as a blueprint for other landowners to copy, creating a valued and sought-after wild dog population.

As with the BioBoundary Project in Botswana, the development of wild dog tourism ventures is evidence of how conservation bodies are working to find ways to establish a place for the wild dog in a developing continent. Alongside such efforts, the arrival of two dogs in the Tuli region of Botswana from 450 kilometres away in eastern Zimbabwe shows just how resourceful these animals are and that it is not too late to reverse the diminishing population. Of course, there are natural factors affecting wild dog numbers. For millennia, lions have made wild dogs underdogs in nature but it is only in the last 100 years or so that we have made wild dogs underdogs in existence. Their continuing decline is on our watch and this was made abundantly clear in early 2011 when Stellar, her new alpha mate and one of their pups were all killed in snares on Mkhuze Game Reserve within the same week that the alpha female on Hlambanyathi Game Reserve was shot by poachers.

An uncertain road ahead *(right): The wild dog's future remains in the balance. While numbers continue to fall, efforts are being made to change our way of thinking about this sociable predator.*

Big business *(overleaf): Africa's 'Big Five' is a marketing success story and has made an African safari a must-do holiday experience. But, has the micro-management of small game reserves intent on providing guests with views of these most famous of African beasts been to the detriment of other species like the African wild dog?*

Acknowledgements

Finding and photographing such a wide-roaming endangered species at various locations across South Africa and Botswana required careful planning. This project simply wouldn't have got off the ground without the vast knowledge and help of Harriet Davies-Mostert of the Endangered Wildlife Trust (EWT) and Chairperson of the Wild Dog Advisory Group in South Africa, and I am eternally grateful.

Whenever I was following African wild dogs through the bush, be it on foot or in a Land Rover, the best motto always seemed to be to expect the unexpected. One never quite knew what these highly energetic and unpredictable animals were going to do next. The opportunities for photography that did materialise were largely due to the field skills and intimate understanding of wild dog behaviour of John Power, Brendan Whittington-Jones and Wendy Collinson of EWT, and of Craig Jackson of the Northern Tuli Predator Project. Above and beyond helping me in my quest, professionalism and a commitment to the research and wellbeing of their canid subjects flowed through each of these dedicated individuals.

My thanks also to Sithembiso Ndlovu for affording me the opportunity to witness the work being done by EWT to educate communities in rural areas about the African wild dog and its importance. Community engagement work is vital to the fight to find a place for endangered species in a modern world but it is all too often undercelebrated.

Various other experts have been instrumental in helping me to piece together the story of the wild dog's past and understand the wider landscape of wild dog conservation. These include Dr Rosemary Groom of the Lowveld Wild Dog Project in eastern Zimbabwe and Kath Potgieter of EWT in South Africa. Also, painting a picture of man's historical relationship with the wild

dog in Southern Africa would not have been possible without the input of archaeologist Tim Forssman of Oxford University.

Beyond my thanks to him for showing his belief in the project by penning the foreword, I also extend my gratitude to Professor Peter Neville for his great friendship and support.

A sincere word of thanks to Warwick Davies-Mostert at the De Beers Venetia Limpopo Nature Reserve for his welcoming hospitality. My appreciation also to staff at Botswana's Mashatu Game Reserve and at KZN Wildlife's Hluhluwe Imfolozi Park and Mkhuze Game Reserve.

I wouldn't be doing the work I love if it wasn't for the unending belief of my family and the inspiration of friends, for which I feel very lucky.

Finally, to share time and space with various wild dog packs, watch their intimate moments and follow them hunting was a true and rare privilege. These are moments that I hope every person who reads this will one day enjoy. Thanks to the help and work of Justine, Peter and Barbara at NatureBureau, I have been able to make *Underdogs* a reality and ensure that every person who buys this book will be helping to secure a future for the African wild dog.